THE TROUBLE *with* CHRISTIANITY

A CONCISE OUTLINE OF CHRISTIAN HISTORY:
FROM THE TRADITIONAL WESTERN BIRTH
OF CHRIST (PBUH) TO CONTEMPORARY
AMERICAN EVANGELICAL FUNDAMENTALISM

Philip Voerding

authorHOUSE®

AuthorHouse™
1663 Liberty Drive
Bloomington, IN 47403
www.authorhouse.com
Phone: 1-800-839-8640

First published by AuthorHouse   8/24/2009

ISBN: 978-1-4389-8924-2 (sc)
ISBN: 978-1-4389-8944-0 (hc)

Printed in the United States of America
Bloomington, Indiana

This book is printed on acid-free paper.

Contents

Acknowledgement

I wish to thank the brothers and sisters who aided me in editing and publishing this book, by the grace of Allah. First of all, I would like to thank Odeh Muhawesh, who has published books in English and Arabic, and who is currently an adjunct professor at the University of St. Thomas in St. Paul, Minnesota, for his guidance and teaching and for the input he gave me while I was writing this book. Secondly, I would like to thank Khaled Sharafuddin, for keeping after me to complete this book, and for taking over as the editor of this project. Thirdly, I would like to thank Ahmad Yassine, Shane Oborn and Christopher Hawes, for their help on this project. Lastly, I would like to thank my wife Josefina for her understanding and her practical advice, and for her support of the project.

"And whatever good they do, they will not be denied the meed thereof. Allah is Aware of those who ward off (evil)." Quran 3:115

Introduction

In the Name of Allah, the Compassionate, the Merciful

A few years after I became a Muslim by the grace of Allah at the age of 39, some of my brothers in Islam suggested that I write a book explaining how and why I became a Muslim and, for that matter a "12er" Shia Muslim. Since I had never written a book until now, this seemed to be an overwhelming task. Finally, in the autumn of 2005, I began to write this book. Since I work a full-time job and have a family, including my twin boys Odeh and Adam (who will turn four years old within a month, Allah willing), it took about a year to finish this book. Everything that is good about this book is from Allah, and all of the mistakes are mine.

To begin this book, I ought to introduce myself. I was born in 1960 C.E. in Great Lakes, Illinois and baptized into the Roman Catholic Church. I remember going to church at a very young age, but since Mass was in Latin, I don't remember much about what it was like. In 1965, my father, who served 20 years in the United States Navy, brought the family to the state of Virginia. I remember that I was not taken to Sunday Mass during the two years we lived there. However, when we returned to Minnesota, where both of parents were originally born, they began to take me to Mass every week. The Mass was now in English, and I enjoyed attending them. My father bought me a copy of the Peoples Mass Book, which also contained hymns. I remember memorizing the Mass and singing the hymns in the evenings after school. When I made my first Holy Communion[1], my family had a get-together at our home. It was a bright, sunny Sunday and my aunts, uncles and cousins came for lunch. I was dressed in a suit. As an eight-year-old boy, I thought it was the best day of my life.

Two years later in 1970, I made my Confirmation. My uncle (who had traveled from Minnesota to Illinois to be my Godfather at my Baptism in 1960) was my sponsor. However, as wonderful as the ceremony was, going to Mass was not as wonderful as it had been a few years earlier--that was because Mass had changed. All the prayers I had memorized were changed and

---

[1] i.e. coming up to the Altar and kneeling down while the priest put the tasteless consecrated wafer of wheat on my tongue

usually simplified. During the "Canon" of the Mass, when the priest changed the bread and wine into the "Body and Blood" of Christ, I liked to hear the names of Apostles, Saints and early Popes. However, shorter Canons had been introduced and those prayers were for the most part omitted. Of course, my Peoples Mass Book was now obsolete. A small digest-sized magazine was now provided in the pews every few months. For me, going to Mass was never the same. My father actually quit attending Mass not just because of the changes, but also because he didn't see how a "guitar Mass" with folk-singers could be a real Mass. My mother, however, continued to faithfully attend Mass, which she did for the rest of her life, God bless her soul.

The changes to Mass were, as I learned years later, just one example of sweeping changes brought about in the Roman Catholic Church by the 21st Ecumenical Council, Vatican II. Pope John XXIII who became the Supreme Pontiff after the death of Pope Pius XII wanted to "open the windows" of the Church to "let in some fresh air." What this meant for Mass was that the Liturgy was celebrated in the vernacular language rather than the official Church language, Latin. Then, the Mass itself was changed; it seemed to make the Liturgy easier for Protestants to accept. While it is true that some Protestants did eventually become Roman Catholics as a result, many Roman Catholics, such as my father, quit attending Mass. Some later ended up becoming Protestants. Others became Fundamentalist Evangelicals. Some, as a result of the Charismatic Movement being allowed to flourish in the Catholic Church, joined Pentecostal churches.

As for me, I quit attending Sunday Mass with my mother at about the age of 13 or 14. My father did send me to Catholic schools for all of my junior and senior high school years. However, I was now a teenager and not much interested in the Church any longer.

Then, in the spring of my junior year in high school, a friend of mine invited me to his church as a guest one Sunday. He and his family attended an "Independent and Fundamentalist" Baptist Church. I decided to accept the invitation and was surprised by Sunday Worship service at this Baptist Church. There was no Mass and no regular prayers. Instead, the congregation would sing several songs. Then, ushers would collect the tithes and offerings from the congregation. This was followed by 'special music.' The main portion of the service was the hour-long sermon that followed the 'special music.' I found it a bit amusing that the preacher would say, "I'm going to close with this last point" and then preach on this point as long as he had the earlier points of his sermon. The service would end with several invitations for those who had not yet accepted Jesus as their Savior to come up and pray and be 'born again' at the altar, while the organist and the congregation sang the verses of the hymn "Just as I am (without one plea)." I had never imagined that church could ever be like this, a simple and non-liturgical worship service!

After that first Sunday, I attended the next two Sundays and found myself actually responding to the invitation at the end of the service, making a profession of faith, and joining the Baptist Church. Not long afterward, I was baptized again because, as the preacher had said, one needs to accept Jesus as Savior of his or her own free will before being baptized. Thus, my Catholic baptism didn't count. Needless to say, my uncle, who had been my Godfather, was not happy. He boldly declared, "You weren't a good Catholic, and you won't be a good Baptist." That comment really stung me at the time.

The youth pastor at the Baptist church took me under his wing and suggested I buy a copy of the King James translation of the Bible. The pastor and many of the members owned a copy of the Scofield Reference Bible using the King James translation. I also learned that 'born again' Christians would be raptured and meet Jesus Christ 'in the air' before the Seven Year Tribulation period when the anti-Christ would persuade the Jews and Palestinians to sign a peace treaty with him. The anti-Christ would be the ruler of a One-World government that would eventually force every person of the world to receive the Mark of the Beast in order to buy and sell (participate in the World Economy). The peace treaty would be broken by the Anti-Christ after three-and-half years, at which point the Great Tribulation would begin. Anyone who did not bear the Mark of the Beast would be killed. God would punish the world during this time. I was told that 144,000 Jews would be saved, as well as those who were also children at the Rapture, if they later became Born Again Christians. The armies of the world would attack the anti-Christ at the Battle of Armageddon in Israel. During the battle, Jesus Christ would return to defeat all these armies and set up his Millennial Kingdom to rule the Earth with a rod of iron. No born-again Christians needed fear, because they would be raptured out of the world before the Tribulation period, and any who died before that time would go to heaven because they were eternally secure and could not lose their salvation.

I attended this Baptist Church for about one year, but eventually attended less and less, by the summer of 1978 I had quit attending altogether. I still had my Bible and was eternally secure, or so I thought. Almost a year later, I met some Christians who attended the Assembly of God Church. They said they were Pentecostals. My youth pastor at the Baptist Church had warned me about Pentecostals because they "spoke in tongues" and acted very emotional and were wild. I didn't think the Christians who attended the Assembly of

God Church were wild and emotional, but they did speak in tongues, and that bothered me. They also taught that one could lose one's salvation by living in sin, which at the time I didn't want to hear. After meeting these Pentecostals, sad to say, I became less interested in the things of God and went about my worldly ways, believing I was eternally secure, until the spring of 1985.

A childhood friend of mine had become a born-again Christian and started attending a Pentecostal holiness church. His mother and my mother were childhood friends who attended the same Catholic parish that my mother and father would attend when I was a child. My friend's mother was not happy at all that he had left the Catholic Church. My friend also knew that I had left the Catholic Church and later attended a Baptist Church. Thus, when he learned that I was no longer a member of that Church, he took it upon himself to "win me back to Christ."

My friend would call me and ask if I wanted to hang out with him after coming home from work. When we would get together, he would warn me that I was not living my life for the Lord and that I should repent of my sins and turn back to Christ, start going to church again and start reading the Bible again. After a while, when my friend would call, I would say I was busy that night. My friend would then keep me on the phone for an hour and tell me what his pastor had preached about the Sunday before. I could never find it in my heart to tell my friend not to call me, so I would have my brother or sister answer the phone if I thought my friend would be calling. I'd have my brother and sister say, "Philip is not home." My persistent friend realized that I was trying to avoid him. Thus, he would show up at my house without any warning. Of course, he was my friend, so I could never tell him to leave. My brother informed me once that sometimes my friend would come to the house when I was away, and then my brother would get the sermon!

After several months, my friend realized that his efforts to 'win my soul' weren't working. One day, after not seeing my friend for a few weeks, he showed up at my door. This time, he asked if I wanted to go to the deli, just down the street, for dinner. When he saw me frown, he said, "Philip, I know that you are uncomfortable when I come over because I always talk to you about the Gospel. So, I've decided that when I come over, I won't talk about the Gospel anymore. I still want to be your friend even if you don't want to come to church with me or study the Bible with me." I could see that my friend meant what he said, and so we started hanging out together more often.

After a few weeks, my friend said to me, "I know I said I wouldn't talk about the Gospel anymore, but Easter Sunday is coming up and I want to invite you to come to church just for Easter." I remember that I didn't feel pressured and thought to myself that it couldn't hurt, so I agreed to come to his church for Easter.

I can still remember what it was like that Easter Sunday at my friend's church, which was called 'Good Shepherd.' It was an independent Pentecostal Holiness Church. The worship service began with handclapping Gospel songs, then medium temple hymns and also a slow chorus. People were clapping, lifting their hands to heaven, and after the songs ended one would hear "Alleluia" and "Praise the Lord!" The majority of the people in attendance were my age (25 at the time) or a bit older, but not more than 10 years older. After the offering, there was special music. Then the pastor began to preach. I was not ready for what I was about to hear. At the Baptist Church, I had heard sermons where the pastor mainly said "do this and don't do that" and might tell a long story to go along with instruction, asking us to turn in our Bibles to a particular verse that went along with the instruction. Everything always seemed to be in the New Testament, and usually in one of Paul's epistles. The sermons at the Assembly of God Church were similar, except that there was no yelling and the message tended to be presented more positively.

However, the sermon I heard at Good Shepherd quoted scriptures from the Old and New Testament. The instruction seemed to be more thorough than I had heard in the previous settings. There was very little yelling, and then only when an important point needed to be made. I became uncomfortable during the sermon because the pastor seemed to be 'reading my mail,' so to speak. The message he was preaching seemed to be meant for me personally. I knew that I was not where God wanted me to be. And yet, a part of me was rejecting what I was hearing. I thought to myself: I believe in God, I had faith in Jesus Christ, what more do I need? The answer was that I needed to turn away from my worldly life and submit unto God, or in my thinking at this time, submit to Jesus as Lord. After the sermon was over, I was relieved because I wasn't being challenged in my heart anymore.

As a result of the sermon, I found myself wanting to find my Bible, which I hadn't touched in almost five years. At first, I only read the historical commentary between the Old and New Testaments. However, soon I was reading some of the study notes. I saw some verses I never saw before because I had previously only read those parts of the Bible that I had underlined during sermons at the Baptist Church. I found several verses I didn't know about previously that clearly suggested it was possible to lose one's salvation. A sense of anxiety came over me because of these verses listed in the study notes of the Bible. In fact, I became frightened and cried out to God to save me. Just saying those words helped me to calm down, and within a few minutes I decided I didn't have to be so worried about my condition. But I realized that things in my mind weren't the same now as before I read the study notes, so I promised God I would read three chapters of the Bible every night before I went to bed, which made the lingering anxiety subside into the background of my mind.

Within two weeks of making my promise to God that I would read three chapters of the Bible before going to bed, I suddenly found myself wanting to attend Church and to quit smoking cigarettes. Soon, I was getting rid of things that I believed were negative in my life. Besides attending Church on Sundays, I wanted to take the "Discipleship Class" for new Christians. Very soon, I was a member of Good Shepherd Church, which made my friend very happy.

I attended Good Shepherd from 1985 to the beginning of 1993. The church ran a 3-Year Bible Institute for training pastors, missionaries, church workers, and anyone else who wanted to attend. In 1988, I received my diploma from Good Shepherd Bible Institute. Later, I would take other courses from another Pentecostal Bible Institute, and then go through lectures presented to Christian workers in a group called Agape Force, a mildly Pentecostal, holiness ministry that actually wanted well-rounded Christian education and offered classes on Theology and presented some philosophy and even psychology. At Good Shepherd, I knew for instance, about Calvinists (who seemed to be Determinists), and Arminians (who seemed to believe in Free-Will). Other than this, I really didn't learn much about these theologies, and so I had many misconceptions based upon my ignorance of their doctrinal systems.

In 1991, I married my first wife, a divorcee who had three children from a previous marriage. When this woman had become a Christian, her husband left her for the woman with whom he had been having an affair. Despite being the sister-in-law of the pastor, my ex-wife did not have a good experience at Good Shepherd. Thus, at the beginning of 1993, we began to attend a mission church of the non-Pentecostal Holiness denomination of the Church of God, headquartered at Anderson Seminary in Anderson, Indiana. That same fall, I was appointed to the Elder Board of the Church, called Heartland Community Church. Here, I began a significant study of Christian history and dogma.

I had read the book: Lectures on the Revival of Religion and An Abridgement of the Biography of Charles Grandison Finney, at Good Shepherd. While at Heartland, I learned that Finney, a controversial but successful evangelist and later seminary professor and anti-Mason activist, had also written a Systematic Theology and also had outlined a course of theological lectures. Good Shepherd did not recommend theological study during the time I attended. From Finney, I learned about doctrines held by Evangelical Christians before the rise of Fundamentalism in the first decade of the 20th century. Finney described God as a Benevolent and Moral Governor who was just and merciful and governed wisely for the highest good of the subjects of His creation. Previously, I had been taught that God's justice was at odds with His mercy. God as presented by Charles Finney is a God who had designed physical and moral laws according to His love. A law without a punishment is merely good advice, and therefore God punishes unrepentant sinners for the highest good of His creation, since the unrepentant are not moved to do good just by being given good advice.

I believe to this day that some of the points Finney made in Systematic Theology changed the way I viewed God and His purposes. In fact, Finney's influence most likely led me to choose 12er Shia Islam over Sunni Islam. Theodicy, the justice of God, became a very important facet of God's activities in my understanding.

Soon, I learned that Finney's Moral Government Theology was the final result of concepts first explored in the writings of Jonathan Edwards, the 18th century evangelist and theologian who is still considered by many to be America's finest Christian theologian. Edwards' ancestors were early Puritans, so his theology was Reformed and Calvinist, as opposed to John Wesley, the Anglican priest to whom the Methodist Churches are heir. Wesley was an Arminian in theology. Learning this led me to study the doctrines of the Reformed faith, which led me to read about Martin Luther and John Calvin on the one hand, and Jacob Arminius and Hugo Grotius on the other. I found that Luther and Calvin were influenced by Augustine of Hippo who wrote back in the late 4th and early 5th centuries C.E. Arminius was less Augustinian than either Luther or Calvin. Arminians held views similar to what theologians call Semi-Pelagianism. Grotius studied the early eastern Catholic Church fathers like John Cassian and Gregory of Nazianzus. Thus, the Calvinist-Arminian debate I learned about at Good Shepherd was just the Protestant version of Augustinian-Eastern Christian debates from the 4th and 5th Centuries. I had thought that modern Pentecostalism had restored the 1st Century Church when actually arguments within Pentecostalism and

Evangelicalism that persist into the 21st century have their roots in the 4th and 5th century! That was quite an eye-opener for me! (In the main section of this book I will go into more details about these Christians and their schools of doctrine).

In 1995, Heartland Community Church merged with another Church of God fellowship. This is because Heartland, which was a suburban mission church, only attempted to reach the unchurched residents of the eastern suburbs of my city and did not subscribe to the philosophy that one build a big new church building to attract other Christians who may begin to attend. Instead, Heartland began by meeting in a high school and remained there for the six or seven years of its existence. When some key families, including mine, moved out of the area, Heartland's congregation no longer could bring in enough money to pay the bills.

Two years as an Elder of a church was enough for me. I liked the pastor and the other Elders, but dealing with the congregation was another matter. Our church government at Heartland was of the kind that we could have passed through what we wanted as Elders of the church, while the congregation had no real input. However, we wanted to be sensitive to the wishes of the congregation. Thus, the Elders decided to put the idea to the congregation to go to a house-church format (which would allow us to save the money that went to the cost of renting space in the high school every Sunday, thus giving us the money to pay the full-time pastor). We discussed our plan with the congregation and even put the plan to a vote. Although the plan had some support, the congregation voted to continue meeting in the high school. As a result of the vote, a couple of families who supported the house church idea left Heartland because "the Elders won't do what God wants them to do!" Thus, we had to ask the pastor to either work part-time, or find a new pastor willing to do so.

About this time, I bought my first copy of a translation of the Quran. This was Muhammad Marmaduke Pickthal's translation. Previously, in fact as early as 1986, I had worked with Muslims and had befriended them. I had tried to share the Gospel as I understood it with my Muslim co-workers, but I never would get anywhere with them. Instead of arguing with me, as other kinds of Christians might do, they just smiled. I remember that one of the brothers, Mahmoud, emigrated from Eritrea, asked me why Christians eat pork. I responded that in the Book of Acts of the Apostles, Simon Peter had a dream where God showed him unclean animals and told Peter to arise, kill and eat, because whatever God has made is clean. Just thinking of that time makes me chuckle, because it sounds so amusing to me today. But I was serious at the time. Mahmoud just smiled at my answer. Of course, Peter was having the dream because the Gospel was to be preached to the Gentiles for the first time, and both Peter and God interpreted the dream to mean that Gentiles were not unclean and so the Gospel could be preached to them. Imagine telling a Muslim that the apostle Peter received a legal ruling from a dream!

The Quran turned out to be a decidedly different book than what I had been led to believe by various evangelical fundamentalist Christian "cult" experts. I had read that one would not be able to understand the Quran because it was not written historically "like the Bible." However, Pickthal included in his introduction to his translation a short summary of the life of the prophet Muhammad (PBUH)[2] and explained what was meant by "an early Meccan Surah," "a late Meccan Surah," and "a Medina Surah." I didn't have much of a problem placing the Surahs (as the chapters of the Quran are called) into the outline of Prophet's life. I also found that the message of the Quran was clear and consistent throughout. I was a strong Christian at that time but I still found myself pleasantly surprised by the Quran. As a result, I decided to try and get more information.

I went online into IRC (Internet Relay Chat) and found a Muslim channel. There, in the forum, I started asking questions. An African-American Sunni sister who said she had been raised Nation of Islam but in college had become Sunni Muslim answered my questions. She informed me that I couldn't learn about Islam just by reading the Quran. I needed to find an Islamic Scholar and study authentic Islamic traditions and the four Schools of Practice. The sister also gave me the name of an African American brother at the University of Minnesota who could get me some books. This brother was very helpful giving me some basic books on (Sunni) Islam. Another brother sent me a copy of the Summarized "Sahih (authentic) of Bukhari," one of the compilers of Sunni Islamic traditions. I was also able to borrow some books on Sunni Hadeeth Science. I also read a short history of Islam.

After reading these books, I concluded that Sunni Hadeeth Science left something to be desired because even if all the Companions of the Prophet and their narrators were all good Muslims, which I found hard to believe considering what I had read about early Islamic history and by the Quranic references to hypocrites among the Muslims, all the Companions and transmitters of Hadeeth would have to be infallible in each narration. Not even the Pope is always infallible, but only claims to be so when he makes

---

[2]   Short for peace be upon him/her.

an Ex Cathedra (from the chair "of Peter" – the first Pope) statement that is worded in the proper manner. Also, I couldn't bring myself to accept that some of the 'authentic' traditions in the Summarized Bukhari were really authentic. The example that always comes to my mind is the one where the Prophet (PBUH) suggests that some people drink camel urine. I didn't believe the one who revealed the Quran would suggest someone should do that!

As a result, I didn't continue investigating Islam at that time. However, I did from time to time read the Quran. Also, in a used bookstore, I found a copy of Idries Shah's book "Thinkers of the East" which introduced me to Sufism. I found the Sufi stories interesting and entertaining reading. Thus, from time to time, I would also read a book on Sufism.

My family had moved out of the area at the same time Heartland merged with another local Church of God congregation. It was just as well, because my studies in the history of Christian dogma had led me to conclude that all the important dogmas of Christianity go back to the early Church. However, the early Catholic Church didn't exist as such anymore. There was the Roman Catholic Church, the Eastern Orthodox Church, the Anglican Church, and various Eastern Churches that had separated from the early Catholic Church in the 4th and 5th centuries C.E. Thus, in early 1996, I began to visit an OCA (Orthodox Church in America) Parish.

Before attending the Divine Liturgy, I read "The Orthodox Church" by Timothy Ware. Even after reading Ware's book, I wasn't prepared for the beauty of Divine Liturgy of St. John Chrysostom. The choir was so beautiful and the melodies were so rich! I remember I wasn't sure what to think about the icons I saw in the parish I visited. I saw Orthodox Christians lighting candles and praying toward the icons. The Orthodox say that they are actually asking the saints to pray for them, and that the icons are "windows into heaven" and therefore just tools of worship. But that explanation didn't make me feel much better. At the time, I wasn't bothered by the icons themselves, but what the people in the church were doing in front of the icons.

I spent a few months attending the OCA Orthodox parish which happened to be only three blocks away from my childhood home. The priest (a convert to Orthodoxy himself) began instructing me in the basic teachings of Orthodoxy. One day when he was doing some work in the sanctuary, I made an offhand comment that it was so good to attend an ancient liturgy rather than the Roman Catholic Mass. The priest responded with a funny look and then told me that the traditional Latin Mass was actually more ancient than the current form of the Divine Liturgy of St. John Chrysostom. That caught me by surprise at the time, but I realize now that during the time I spent at Good Shepherd, I had developed an anti-Roman Catholic prejudice. The priest also told me that he believed the Roman Catholic Church and the Eastern Orthodox Churches would eventually somehow reunite, although some centuries would probably pass in the meantime.

I can remember thinking to myself that the Roman Catholic Church must not be so bad after all. For the next few days I thought about when I was a child attending Mass, praying the Rosary with my grandmother when I was five and six years old and walking to Mass with my mother when I was 11 or 12 years old. Perhaps the Roman Catholic Church and the Eastern Orthodox Church are really two branches of the same church. If that's true, since I was raised a Roman Catholic, perhaps God wanted me to attend there, where I could go to Mass with my mother. Thus, I decided to go with my mother to Mass the next week.

My mother had attended the same parish since she was born. Before Vatican II, this had been what was called a 'National Parish,' as opposed to a 'Diocesan Parish.' The Diocesan Parish was under the authority of the local bishop, but the National Parish was under a different authority (though I can't remember all the details of how that worked anymore). The patron saint of the parish was St. Ambrose, whose preaching had helped to influenced Saint Augustine to leave the 'heretical' sect of the Manicheans for the Catholic Church. Saint Ambrose had been a parish attended by Italian families. After Vatican II and in fact until the parish was moved to a suburb in the late 1990s, the parish was distinctly an Italian parish, with almost half the membership still Italian at the time that the building was sold and the parish re-established. I have been told by conservative Catholic experts of Canon Law that the move actually violated canonical law, since the parish is the actual area of land that is served by the building and its ordained clergy. But the move was allowed by the Archbishop nonetheless. However, the announcement of the move was two years in the future.

My mother was very happy that I came to Mass with her. It had been about twenty years since I had attended Mass with my mother. The altar had been removed and replaced by a table, a development of Vatican II, but the same priest (whom I liked very much as a child) was still the pastor. In fact, the same commentator, an Italian American with a good speaking voice, still gave the readings. It was almost like being seven years old again. I remember that I enjoyed the Mass. Out of curiosity, I asked the priest how one who had not attended mass for twenty years but had joined another church could return to the Catholic Church, and the priest responded that one would have to go to confession, but that if I wanted to do that I should meet with him first. I did some soul searching, and after a few days, I made an appointment to see the priest. We talked about why I left the Catholic Church, where I attended in the meantime, and why I had come back. The priest was very happy to see me return. The priest had only positive things to say about the Eastern Orthodox Church, which again was a surprise for me. As a result of the appointment, I decided to return to the Roman Catholic Church. Since I liked the Eastern liturgy, I could also attend Eastern Roman Catholic rites if I wanted. That had been changed by Vatican II, also.

The only problem that came up in returning to the Roman Catholic Church was my marriage. My wife had previously been married in the Church. She was divorced from her husband but still married in the Church according to Canonical Law. Pre-Vatican II, the solution would have been that there was no true marriage between my wife and me. We could live together as brother and sister, sleeping in different rooms. Under the new canonical law however, this diocese would probably grant my wife an annulment, although her specific case would have to be reviewed. Then, we would be allowed to marry. In the meantime, we could only live together as brother and sister.

My wife, who later became my ex-wife, was not attending any church. She still remembered the bad experiences she had in churches she had attended after becoming a born-again Christian. She had been hurt from her previous marriage. Also, the fact that her three boys, now teenagers, did not get along well with me, had been a great disappointment for her. She did not want to go through the annulment process. All of these problems had caused us to grow apart in our relationship. Neither of us was happy. So, after thinking it over for three months of living as brother and sister instead of as husband and wife, we decided to get a divorce. We both felt a great relief and actually became friendlier with each other as a result of the decision. Even the relationship between her children and I improved. Although sad and disappointed because the marriage hadn't worked out, I was free to marry in the Roman Catholic Church.

I will briefly summarize the next few years as a Roman Catholic. As apparent from what I previously wrote about the Church, I found myself moving toward the conservatives and traditionalists within the Church. I preferred to attend Mass on Sundays at the parish that performed the new Mass in a solemn setting as well as the parish that had permission to celebrate the Traditional Latin Mass. At times I would visit the Byzantine, Ukrainian, and Maronite Catholic liturgies. Although the Society of Saint Pius X chapels were considered to be out of communion with Rome after the late Archbishop Lefebvre canonized bishops without the authority of the Vatican so that society would continue to be able to ordain priests after he passed away, I even attended Mass at their chapels. Frankly, their celebration of the Mass of the Western Rite appealed to me the most. I came very close to exclusively attending the SSPX chapels, but in the end, obeyed the authority of the Church.

For several years I had a job which allowed me to do a lot of reading at work with the approval of my supervisors. While a Roman Catholic, I read several books on Catholic history and dogma. Among these were Ludwig Ott's Catholic Dogma, both the Catechism of the Council of Trent and the modern Catechism of the Catholic Church, as well as Denzinger's Sources of Catholic Dogma (which lists all the historic documents that were used in forming Catholic Dogma throughout the centuries), books on the development of the Roman Mass, criticisms of the Reformation, and early Church history. It was the last category of books, those dealing with the first few centuries of the Church, which began to cause problems for me.

I had always believed that dogmas outlined in the Nicene-Constantinopolitan Creed and the Definition of Chalcedon (formulated during the first four Ecumenical Councils of the Catholic Church) was the way by which most Christians had always confessed Orthodox belief. I knew about Marcion and his short canon of Scripture (ten letters of the apostle Paul and an edited Gospel of Luke), but I didn't know his movement was such a threat to early Orthodox Christianity (what some scholars call the Proto-Orthodox). Also, I never realized that the doctrine of the Trinity had developed from the time the term was coined, by the early Latin Church Father Tertullian to the late 4th century C.E. Then I learned that the one who coined the term Trinity was not canonized as a saint because he had become a Montanist (another early Christian sect considered heretical by the Catholic Church), and then lastly formed his own little sect. There were so many sects in early Christianity!

The various sects that were categorized as Gnostic did not bother me at the time, although I was fascinated by them, which led me to obtain a copy of the Nag Hammadi documents translated into English. What did bother me was learning about Jewish Christian sects such as the Ebionites and Nazoreans. Though some of these sects had a Gnostic influence, here were Torah-Observant followers of Jesus Christ, some of whom not only rejected Paul's apostleship but also the deity of Christ! This non-Pauline Jewish Christianity looked more than a little bit like Islam to me!

During the summer of 1998, I began reading books on Sufism again, and came across sayings of Jesus from Sufi sources. Later, I found a collection of these online from the book Christ in Islam compiled by James Robson (which I have learned is in print again, but has been superseded by the books The Muslim Jesus by Tarif Khalidi and Jesus through Shia Narrations by Mahdi Muntazir Qa'im and Muhammad Legenhausen). The few sayings I was able to read at the time portrayed a Jesus (PBUH) both similar to the Jesus I found in the Quran and to the Jesus of the early Jewish Christian sects.

Around that same time, I came across a book with the surprising title, The Mythmaker: Paul and the Invention of Christianity written by Hyam Maccoby. If I had not known about the Ebionites by this time, I might have dismissed Maccoby's title alone as anti-Christian propaganda. Instead, the title intrigued me, and so I purchased the book. As much as I did not want to believe what Maccoby had to say, the book had the effect over time of persuading me to lose trust in the Pauline Epistles as inspired scripture. When I read the Quran the first time, at one point I did begin to wonder why Judaism was a strictly monotheistic religion in most of its forms, just like Islam, but orthodox Christianity held the doctrines of the Trinity, the Deity of Jesus, and the Crucifixion for the forgiveness of sins. I had been able to shake that question off without much problem previously, but after reading Maccoby's book, the question would come back to me again and again because of the doubts I now had about Paul. Was Paul a true apostle or a false apostle?

In the autumn of 1998, I came across another book that would have a lasting effect on me. While shopping in a used book store, I came across a copy of A Short History of Islam by S. F. Mahmud. There are probably better books on Islamic history from a Sunni perspective, but in the early chapters, Mahmud describes the wars at the time of the early Muslim caliphate. I had read a book on Islamic history once before, but the way Mahmoud positively described Ali Ibn Abu Talib (PBUH) and his son Hussein Ibn Ali (PBUH) caught my attention. But then, Mahmoud went on to say that the Shia Muslims look to these two as their leaders, yet he did not accept aspects of Shia belief and practice. It seemed to me that, with the beginning of the Umayyad caliphate, the Muslim state came under less than optimum leadership. Furthermore, what little I knew or had heard about Shia Muslims was very negative. How could that be if they had the better leaders? Although at the time it was barely more than an intellectual pursuit, I wanted to learn more about who the Shias really are. But I wasn't thinking about more than that at the time.

I didn't know any Shia Muslims; so again, I had to go online to find some. A few months later, I finally found a place where Shia Muslims chatted online. The chat room conversation seemed to be that of teenagers talking about things teenagers usually talk about, but I wrote to the channel that I was a Christian who wanted to learn more about Shia Muslims. A "12er" Shia Muslim sister, who had previously not been conversing, responded to my request for information. She took my name, my address, and email address and said she would put me in contact with Shia Muslims and send my address to some Islamic Centers so that I might receive some books. I gave her my contact information and asked some questions and that was that. In the meantime, I looked for information on the internet about Shia Muslims. Sure enough, in about a week, I received the first of several batches of booklets and books from various Islamic centers. Also, an email was sent to me by a Shia Muslim who would eventually become a good friend, later my brother and teacher in Islam: Odeh Muhawesh.

In the week before I received Odeh's email, I was able to learn some things about Shia Muslims. The website I found first was set up by Ithna Asheri or "12er" Shias. I learned that the 12ers followed the "12 Imams" instead of the Sunni Muslim leaders Abu Bakr and Omar. These Imams were descendants of the Prophet Muhammad (PBUH). Instead of the traditional "Five Pillars" of Sunni Islam (bearing witness that there is no god except Allah and Muhammad is the messenger of Allah, Salat, Fasting, Charity, and Hajj); the 12er Shia Muslims described Islam as the "Five Roots of Religion." The Five Roots are: The Oneness of God, the Justice of God, Prophethood, Imamate (Guidance), and the Resurrection. The practices described in the Sunni "Five Pillars" were included under the ten branches of Religion. Thus, while the Sunnis described Islam as a 'way of life,' it seemed to me that the 12er Shias first described Islam as having a particular ideology and secondly the practices or 'way of life' of Islam. This description made more sense to me from an ethical perspective. The problems I had seen previously in Muslim history were not caused by the Prophet and the Twelve Imams (PBUT)[3], for they weren't the political leaders after the murder of the Imam Ali (PBUH), the 4th caliph. I was pleasantly surprised by what I learned.

One of the first books I read on 12er Shia Islam was The Voice of Human Justice written by an Eastern Christian named George Jordac. Theodicy was the most important belief in 12er Shia ideology after the Oneness of God. I found this to be impressive.

---

[3]   Short for peace be upon them.

I also received a copy of Nahjul Balagha or 'Peak of Eloquence' which turned out to be a compilation of sermons, letters, and wisdom sayings by Imam Ali (PBUH). When I glanced at the wisdom sayings, I saw that this was not the first time I had read anything by Imam Ali Ibn Abu Talib (PBUH). Idries Shah's book, Caravan of Dreams, had a tradition by Imam Ali (PBUH), so I knew the Sufis liked him, and I liked the Sufis. But, it seemed that I was getting deeper into Islam than I had planned!

Odeh Muhawesh, who contacted me not long after I chatted with the sister in the Shia chat room, invited me to his office. I have to admit that, although everything I was reading about 12er Shia Islam was positive, reasonable and even beautiful; in the back of my mind I had some concern and even a little bit of fear. Before reading about Imam Ali (PBUH) and Imam Hussein (PBUH) in Mahmud's book, all I knew about Shia Muslims was that the Ayatollah Khomeini had led a successful revolution against America's friend, the Shah (although I didn't know at the time the reasons for the revolution). I already knew about the classic Islamic philosophers Al-Farabi, Avicenna, and Averroes, but I hadn't known then that these three philosophers were Shia Muslims until I began to read about Shia Islam. However, when I finally met Odeh Muhawesh, I knew right away that any concerns or fears were unfounded. Odeh turned out to be a highly educated successful businessman and family man. He was born in Jordan, not Iran. Odeh was genuinely friendly and though quite willing to answer all of my questions about Shia Islam, did not attempt to persuade me to become a Muslim in that same manner that, say, a Pentecostal Holiness Christian would try to "win a soul" for Christ.

Through Odeh, I was able to meet other Shia Muslims. The local community consisted of Shia Muslims who are primarily Arab, Khoja, Iranian, and Pakistani. I had never heard of Khojas before, but they are Shia Muslims whose ancestors were from the Indian subcontinent. Over a century ago, their forefathers had been Hindus who eventually converted to 12er Shia Islam. Khojas are usually merchants, doctors, or lawyers who had no political power in the lands of their origin. Many were living in East Africa, but migrated to America because of the political upheavals in the later decades of the 20th century. I found these Muslims to be very friendly, polite and hospitable not only with myself but with each other. With some Sunni Muslims (though certainly not all), I had noticed that some would have an unfriendly or even mean disposition. However, I didn't notice this tendency with the Shia Muslims.

I continued to read and ask questions. In my experience, it seemed to be one thing to read about Islam, learn new things and admire those things, yet quite another to suddenly find oneself being drawn to Islam. Like many people, I am not someone who likes change. When I began doubting important beliefs and practices within Christianity, it was emotionally tiring and even somewhat depressing. Being a Christian all of my life, I had become emotionally attached to many things about Christianity. I liked traditional Christian music. After returning to the Roman Catholic Church, I had begun to do the Morning Prayer, Evening Prayer, and Compline (prayer with examination of conscience) from the Liturgy of the Hours. On Sunday mornings I loved to go to Mass and then go to lunch afterward. So it was not an easy thing to become a Muslim.

Yet, I had a strong desire to continue exploring 12er Shia Islam. Within a month of meeting 12er Shia Muslims in my community, I was more or less convinced that Muhammad (PBUH) is the Last Prophet, and that true Islam comes from Allah through the Quran and the guidance of the 14 Infallibles (Prophet Muhammad, his daughter Sayida Fatima Al-Zahraa, and the 12 Imams – peace be upon them all). Yet, it took me six months to actually take the step to give the Shahada (the belief that there is no god except Allah and that Muhammad is the Prophet of Allah). The first month was difficult, but afterwards I was so happy and fulfilled being a 12er Shia Muslim.

My family, surprisingly, was very supportive of my decision to become a Muslim. I can remember the jokes my family made (all in good fun) at the first Thanksgiving celebration after I became a Muslim. "Philip, are you sure those potatoes were slaughtered properly?" in reference to a plate of mashed potatoes I was about to eat. My father, who worked as a cook for many years, was familiar with kosher food and so my desire to eat Halal meat didn't seem strange to him. However, as one would suspect, most of my Christian friends were not happy at all about my decision. Some cut me off completely, but others remained friendly, although many of them at first were quite vocal about the "big mistake" they believed I had made becoming a Muslim.

All in all, I didn't have any problems until the tragedy of 9/11. I remarried late September 2001 to a wonderful Filipina woman from the island of Cebu. She has been a Roman Catholic all her life and arrived in the United States on September 5th 2001. She became a Muslim before we married. It was difficult for her because here she was in a new country, and still fairly new to wearing Hijab (head covering). I remember walking into a department store with my wife one or two days after 9/11, only to see my wife receive what I can only describe as hateful stares from customers. When these customers noticed that my wife was walking with me, I usually received the same stares. However, if I walked into the same store without my wife, no one knew that I was a Muslim because I wore western clothes and have the face of an American whose ancestors were Northern European. There were a few times when I wanted to say something to those who were showing their hate, but I always managed to restrain myself, and later even tried giving a gentle smile in return. On one occasion, in 2004, after the hateful stares had become few and far between, my wife came out of a large supermarket with a shopping cart carrying our twin boys (born in 2003). An older woman began yelling at my wife about money. At first, my wife believed the older woman needed to borrow some money and was about to help the woman. It was not money that the woman wanted, however. This woman began to scold my Asian wife (who was wearing Hijab) for coming to the USA to receive benefits (check from WIC) to receive some free groceries. WIC, of course, will give some help with groceries to any American family who has a low income. My twin boys are American citizens just like I am. When my wife alerted me to the woman, I decided to have a word with the woman about the public verbal abuse she had just given to my wife. Not reaching her car before she started driving out of her parking spot, all I was able to do was get her license plate number, which we promptly gave to the police. That was the worse treatment my wife received after 911, so we thank Allah for protecting us from something more dangerous than this incident.

After almost eight years as a Muslim, I have to say that, by the grace of Allah, becoming a 12er Shia Muslim was the best decision I had ever made in my life. Although there are times that I wished I had been able to become a Muslim in my early twenties, I would not have learned very much about Christianity, its history, and its sects. Also, since I did not know any Muslims (let alone 12er Shia Muslims) in my early twenties, the best that was available for me at the time was Christianity. Allah knows best and by His providence I came to be where I am today. I thank Allah for blessing me with a wonderful family and a wonderful community with so many good and true brothers and sisters, and especially for guiding me to Islam.

Even though I became a 12er Shia Muslim, I continued to read books about Sunni Islam, other Shia Muslims, and even a book on the classic Mutazilites. A short list of some books I read include: The Reliance of the Traveler, a classic manual of the Shafie school of Jurisprudence translated by Sheikh Nuh Keller; The Muwatta of Malik; The Biography of the Prophet Muhammad (PBUH) written by Martin Lings; Kitab Al-Tawheed by Sheikh-ul-Islam Muhammad bin Abdul Wahab; and three books by An-Nawawi (his Al-Magasid/Manual of Islam, the Riyadhus Saliheen Hadeeth collection, and the Forty Hadeeth). I also read Ahmadiyyah scholar Maulana Muhammad Ali's book, The Religion of Islam, and a topical collection of Quranic verses and traditions compiled by him.

Even before becoming a Muslim, I read Dr. Rashad Khalifa's Quran translation, The Final Testament, with his appendices and commentary, as well as other works by modern Muslims who only used the Quran. Khalifa had written about, 'the Quranic Miracle of 19' by which he had demonstrated that the Quran was incorruptible. His first translation of the Quran demonstrated that the word Allah and other words appeared in the Quran a multiple of 19 times. After this, he declared that all Islamic Traditions (Hadeeth) were a corrupting influence on Islam. Later, he published a new addition of his Quran translation with two verses removed which he claimed were fabrications. Although not all Muslim influenced by his ideas joined his movement, Khalifa was an important figure in the modern Quran alone movement.

As soon as I was exposed to the 'Quran alone' sects, I could see that such an approach would lead to the same problem seen in Western Christianity since the Protestant Reformation, which is ever-increasing in number of sects and disunity. This disunity results from approaching the Quran subjectively – that is, according to one's limited understanding. I've been there and done that when I was a Christian. There was no point going down that road again. I truly believe Allah had in mind one Islam, not many. Traditions need to be approached with caution, this is certainly true. However, if I were to approach the Quran with only my limited understanding, in every area where there is the possibility of a difference of opinion with other Muslims, and therefore I have no way of knowing whether my understanding is the correct one, or not. Thus, the Quran alone position did not appear realistic to me.

Finally, I would like to say a few things about the concise history which follows this introduction. The purpose of the history is two-fold. First, I wrote about the history so that my brothers and sisters in Islam might learn some basic Christian history and knowledge of the basic beliefs and practice of various Christian sects. The United States, my homeland, is a predominately Christian nation, although in the second half of the 20th century, the nation has become increasingly more secular. The United States grew out of several British (and also Spanish, French, and Dutch) colonies. Several of the British colonies were made up of very religious Christians who fled persecution by the state Church of England. I honestly believe the USA was founded on Biblical and Quranic principles. Many early American leaders were conservative Christians who were not anti-intellectual fundamentalists (a movement which began in the early 20th century, though the roots of the movement might be traced from the years following the American Civil War). Also, several early American Christian leaders were not Trinitarian. Thomas Jefferson edited the New Testament so that the result was more reasonable. Thomas

Jefferson was also quite fond of the Quran. Benjamin Franklin, although not a very religious man himself, wrote that young people should emulate Jesus, Muhammad, and Buddha. George Washington studied theology while in college and doubted the doctrine of the deity of Christ. These three famous American leaders helped to found the United States. Their influence can be found in the Declaration of Independence, the Constitution, and the Bill of Rights. An American Muslim can be proud of the early history of the United States and can work to bring America more in line with her origins without sacrificing anything within true Islam.

Second, I wrote the history as a response to some of the Christians who are only familiar with the history and teachings of their particular Christian sect and as a result don't know very much about other Christian sects. These Christians have not studied Christian history very much. In the example of the Pentecostal Church where I attended in my mid-twenties to early thirties, there were books about Jonathan Edwards, Charles Finney, Charles Haddon Spurgeon, John Wesley, George Whitfield, and others in the church bookstore, but no books about their respective theologies. All of the five names I mentioned above studied and/or wrote books on theology, but our particular church looked down upon the study of theology. When I wanted a book on doctrine, the only book anyone ever suggested was R. A. Torrey's, What the Bible Teaches, but to my surprise, I later learned that R. A. Torrey was a seminary graduate! The word theology comes from two Greek words that mean 'the study of God' or 'words about God' (and the actual words are Theos, which means 'God,' and 'logos' which means 'word'). Thus, it is ludicrous to say, "You don't need theology; you only need God." Charles Spurgeon, whose library held around 15,000 books at his death, had republished the 1689 London Baptist Confession of Faith in the mid-1800s because he wanted to propagate a theology that was both Reformed (Calvinist and Covenantal) and Baptist. But all we knew about were his sermons and Bible commentaries. All of these Christian terms and movements will be discussed in the history that follows.

Some of the main reference books I used in writing the history are:

1. System Theology by Louis Berkhof (the conservative Reformed/ Calvinist scholar of the early and middle 20th century C.E.).

2. History of Christian Doctrine by Louis Berkhof.

3. Systematic Theology by Augustus H. Strong (Baptist Theologian of the late 19th and early 20th Centuries C.E.).

4. Skeletons of a Course of Theological Lecture by Charles Finney (Outlines of his lectures at Oberlin College from the mid-1840s, which I used not only for the theology but for his "proofs" of the Trinity from Hinduism and other polytheistic religions).

5. The Kindness of God our Savior by Gordon C. Olson (who was a 20th Century Arminian Theologian heavily influenced by the New England/New School theology and sermons of Dr. Jonathan Edwards Jr., Nathaniel W Taylor, and Charles G. Finney – this book summaries the history of the various views of the Christian doctrine of the Atonement as previously presented by the late 19th Century C.E. Methodist theologian John Miley in his Systematic Theology).

6. Creeds in the Churches: A Reader in Christian Doctrine from the Bible to the Present by John H. Leith.

7. Documents of the Christian Church by Henry Bettenson.

8. Oxford Dictionary of Popes by J. N. D. Kelly.

9. Earliest Christian Heretics by Arland J. Hultgren and Steven A. Haggmark.

10. Early Church Fathers (Library of Christian Classics) by Cyril C. Richardson.

11. Christology of the Later Fathers (Library of Christian Classics) by Edward R. Hardy.

12. Here I Stand: A Life of Martin Luther by Roland H. Bainton.

13. The New Testament: A Historical Introduction to the Early Christian Writings by Bart D. Ehrman.

14. The Changing Faces of Jesus by Geza Vermes.

Other books are named in various chapters of the history which follows.

This is the first book I've ever written. I've never tried to do undertake a task like this before. I've attempted to give snapshots of important movements and developments in Christian history. In the future, Allah willing, I may revise the book for readability and for errors that may come to light. One dear brother in Islam, himself a former conservative Evangelical Christian minister, described the book as "a mountain chain of information." Allah willing, it is my hope that this short book will give information to those who read it.

Philip Hamza Ali Voerding
April 25th 2007

"O People of the Scripture! Do not exaggerate in your religion nor utter aught concerning Allah save the truth. The Messiah, Jesus son of Mary, was only a messenger of Allah, and His word which He conveyed unto Mary, and a spirit from Him. So believe in Allah and His messengers, and say not 'Three – Cease! (it is) better for you! – Allah is only One Allah. Far is it removed from His Transcendent Majesty that He should have a son. His is all that is in the heavens and all that is in the earth. And Allah is sufficient as Defender."
Quran 4:171

Preface

History repeats itself. A scholarly study of the split in Jewish society after the deaths of Prophets Moses and Aaron (PBUT) finds that the descendants of Aaron were deprived of leading the Jews and the temple by those who rebelled against them. Two kingdoms were formed, one led by leaders of the rebellion, and another by the legitimate progeny of Aaron. The true followers of Moses' Judaism were cast in a negative light and forced to retreat in fear by the triumphant forces that took over the temple.

Years later, the story was repeated upon the ascension of Jesus Christ (Peace be upon him). Two camps were formed after his departure. One lead by James, his maternal cousin and the legitimate leader assigned by Jesus to lead the believers, and another led by Paul, the self proclaimed recipient of inspiration from Jesus. Like their Jewish predecessors, the triumphant rebels took over the message and shaped the future of Christianity, and forced the righteous followers of God's chosen prophet to retreat into oblivion. In both cases mentioned above, there were several common elements between the leaders of the rebellions and the nature of their actions. In both cases, the rightly chosen heir was a close relative of the Messenger. Aaron was the brother of Moses and it was his children who were charged by Moses to carry the message. James was the maternal cousin of Jesus. Prophet Jesus peace be upon him called James "his brother" exactly as prophet Muhammad called Ali, his cousin, "his brother." The chosen heirs to lead the followers of both prophets were the descendants of Aaron and James respectively. The Jewish rebels' history shows that the leaders were vehement enemies of Moses and Aaron at the beginning of the delivery of the message, and only embraced the new faith after all other attempts to destroy its followers had failed.

By his own admission, Paul was a sworn enemy of Christianity. It was only after the message of Jesus became a reality in that time that Paul suddenly became a devout follower of his aberrational faith which was founded on non-verifiable events. The cases above repeat themselves verbatim in Islam. Prophet Muhammad (Peace be upon him and his progeny) had to face eighty eight battles which were waged against him and his followers. Each one of those battles was designed to annihilate the new religion and its followers. However, when two months before his death, the Prophet assigned Imam Ali, his cousin, as the leader of the Muslim nation by order of the Almighty God, those who embraced Islam after having given up the fight to destroy it realized that they can only win if they stage a coup in step with the Jewish rebels and Paul of Christianity. The leaders of the Muslim rebels had an identical history to Paul. Bernard Shaw in his book "The 100 greatest personalities of all times" states that the resemblance between Paul and Omar was striking.

Judaism, Christianity, and Islam all faced rebellions from within after their sworn enemies were not able to destroy them and have decided to penetrate the leadership after the demise or departure of the patriarchs of each faith. The progeny of a close relative of Moses, Jesus, and Muhammad were systematically killed or exiled, and the followers of the true faith were forced to retreat out of fear for their very existence.

Upon careful and free study of the history of the three major faiths, one can only arrive at the conclusion that the teachings of Moses, Jesus, and Muhammad as revealed to them by God are all the same. Monotheistic, logical, and timeless. All three faiths are truly one and the same with the differences that they were delivered to different people, and different times, by different messengers. All conform to reason and teach that the existence of non-essential beings like humans and all that surround us is a guide to logically conclude that there has to exist an essential being that is one, uncountable, timeless, simple, creator, just, and all knowing. This logic is the corner stone of the teachings of the three great messengers of God, Moses, Jesus, and Muhammad.

All three messengers also taught since the purpose of creation of Adam and his progeny was to have dominion over Earth to worship God alone, a perfect infallible worshiper has to exist at every given moment that Earth itself exists. Thus, each named his heirs until the coming of the messenger, or the end of times in the case of Prophet Muhammad peace be upon him and his progeny, and each messengers heirs hailed from either his brother as in the case of Moses and Aaron, or his cousin as in the cases of Jesus with his cousin James and Muhammad and his cousin Ali. Moreover, the Ten Commandments of Moses, the Sermon on the Mount of Jesus, and the Last Pilgrimage Speech of Muhammad all established the same moral code for humanity.

Brother Philip's journey to the truth as depicted in this very informative work is a navigation through historical, theological, and moral annals of faith that so eloquently and convincingly arrived at the pure faith of the three greatest prophets of God, Moses, Jesus, and Muhammad, peace be upon them all.

Odeh A. Muhawesh

ONE

Palestine in the First Century C.E.

The world into which Christ (PBUH) was born.

Judaism at the time of Christ was not a monolithic religion. Various sects existed within Judaism, yet most Palestinian Jews did not belong to any particular sect. The Priesthood had been sold when Palestine was under the control of the pagan king Antiochus Epiphanes II, over two centuries earlier. This event contributed to the splitting of Palestinian Judaism into several sects.

1. The Sadducee party, which held the High Priesthood, believed in God, the Torah, and not much else. This party always sought good relations with Imperial Rome.

2. The Pharisees remained connected to the temple, but expected all Jews to perform the purifications which the Sadducees believed need only be practiced by the Priesthood.

3. The Essenes broke with the Temple as a result of the selling of the Priesthood.

4. There were Hellenistic Jews (such as Philo) who were influenced by Greek philosophy. A large Hellenistic community existed in Egypt in the First Century C.E.

5. There was the Herodian (or Royalist) party, who supported King Herod (The Great), whose family was actually, from Idumea (an Edomite family).

6. Lastly, there were the Zealots, who resented the Roman occupation so much that they were willing to use force to remove the Romans from Palestine.

In the First Century C.E., Palestine was under the rule of the Roman Empire. Jews who lived in the Roman Empire and in the East made pilgrimages to

Jerusalem during the Jewish Festivals. These non-Palestinian Jews were to some degree influenced by the religion(s) of their host countries. Various Mystery Religions existed in the Greco-Roman world, which would come to have an influence on Christianity, especially among Gentile Christians. Some common features of these 'Mystery Religions' were:

1. Suffering God-men, some of whom came back to life.

2. Voluntary entrance through initiation rites reenacting elements of these myths involving the suffering, death, and rebirth of the God-man for the benefit of the initiate.

3. Healing powers and miraculous abilities possessed by the God-men.

4. Partaking of food and drink by initiates in a ceremony reenacting a holy meal instituted by the God-man of the particular Mystery Religion.

5. Higher level members of the Mystery Religion passed on secret teachings to give the initiated faithful a fuller understanding of the God-man.

6. One could be initiated into more than one Mystery Religion if one so desired.

7. Some Mystery Religions have left no written literature because the religions were reserved for the initiated only, and therefore nothing was written down. Perhaps the best book available on Mystery Religions in general is, "The Ancient Mysteries: A Sourcebook – Sacred Texts of the Mystery Religions of the Ancient Mediterranean World," edited by Marvin W. Meyer.

Platonic and other Hellenistic influences can be seen in Judaism at the time of the traditional birth of Jesus Christ (PBUH). One example can be seen in the writings of Philo of Alexandria (b. 20 B.C.E. – d. 40 C.E.), who was also known as Philo Judeaus. Philo was a Hellenized Jewish philosopher born in Alexandria, Egypt. Philo's philosophy is influenced by both Judaism and the writings of Greek philosophers, such as the Stoics. As a result, Philo's writings were accepted by many early Christians, some of whom actually considered Philo to be a Christian. In "De vita contemplative" (which is Latin for 'The Contemplative Life'), Philo describes the Therapeutae, a Jewish group of ascetics living in the Egyptian desert which some historians have identified with the Essenes. Eusebius, who wrote the Ecclesiastical History in the 4th century C.E., believed that the Therapeutae in Egypt at the time of Jesus Christ (PBUH) were actually a Christian group.

Philo's writings not only show the influence of Stoicism (in such ideas as: 1. The doctrine of God as the only efficient cause, 2. Divine reason immanent in the world, and 3. The doctrine of the Logos), but also Platonism (again, in the belief in the doctrine of the Divine Logos), Pythagorism (in the idea of symbolism in numerology), and Aristotelian metaphysics. Philo's philosophy served the purpose of defending and justifying Jewish religious views in the Greek world.

Jewish Mysticism, according to Kabbalah experts, begins in the Tanakh, the Hebrew scriptures, immediately in the Book of Genesis, especially in the Creation account, the story of Adam (PBUH) and Eve (PBUH), the Garden of Eden, the Tree of the Knowledge of Good and Evil, and the Tree of Life, the relationship of the first humans with the Serpent, and the disaster that followed when they partook of the forbidden fruit. According to tradition, the ancient kabalistic text, Sefer Raziel HaMalach, was revealed to Adam by the angel Raziel after the eviction from Eden. Another ancient kabalistic text, Sefer Yetsira, was supposedly revealed to Abraham (PBUH), according to Jewish mystics. Ancient tradition states that the Kabbalah was given to humans by two angels who fell from heaven, Aza and Azaz'el (or Azaz'el and Uzaz'el). Some scholars believe the oldest versions of Jewish Mysticism come from ancient Assyrian religion and mysticism. The Sepiroth, Tree of Life, in Kabbalism has a general similarity with the Assyrian Tree of Life. There are ten 'emanations of God' or Sephiroth in the kabbalistic Tree of Life.

Kabbalah's antiquity can be seen in ancient Gnosticism. Kabbalistic 'Chochmah' or Wisdom (Greek = Sophia) is an example of Platonic influence, as well as Pythagorean and Stoic ideas, that can be seen in Kabbalistic lore. Jewish Rabbis such as Rabbi Akiva and Ben Zoma distanced themselves from these teachings, which they believed led to heresy. The influence of Zoroastrianism is seen in Kabbalistic Dualism.

TWO

Early Christianity.

The original followers of Christ (PBUH) were Palestinian Jews, the vast majority of whom were raised to keep the Law of Moses (PBUH) – The Torah. The Gospel first preached by Jesus Christ (PBUH), the son of the Blessed Virgin Mary (PBUH), was a Gospel of Repentance from sin and submission toward the One Eternal God, according to the New Testament Gospels. The canonical Gospel of Matthew states that Christ (PBUH) came not to destroy the Law of Moses (PBUH), but to fulfill the Law of Moses (PBUH). Christ (PBUH), the Messiah sent by God to the Jews, used verses from the Torah to show that the law was to be kept in the spirit of compassion, and that true believers ought to love each other as Christ (PBUH) loved the true believers.

The canonical New Testament also has a good amount of writings by Paul (previously Saul) of Tarsus, a Jew who grew up in the city that was the center of the cult of Mithraism, a Mystery Religion popular at the time. Paul did not actually ever meet Jesus Christ before the Ascension, but claimed to have been knocked off of a horse while persecuting Christians during a vision of the Ascended Christ (PBUH). Various scholars have noted that Paul's Gospel of Christ Crucified has similarities to various contemporary Mystery Religions, and also appears to have some influence from Stoicism. The canonical New Testament also states (in the Acts of the Apostles and elsewhere) that Paul at times clashed with the Jerusalem Christian leaders. This is a good indication that Christianity as presented by Paul of Tarsus clashed with the teachings of Jesus Christ (PBUH).

As stated previously, some scholars, ancient and modern, who were critics of the Christianity in the churches that traced their origin from Paul's missionary journeys, believed that the Jesus Christ (PBUH) who was preached by Paul on these missionary journeys was similar to various suffering God-men saviors of the Mystery Religions that existed in Egypt, Greece, Northern Galilee, Syria, Asia Minor, and the Italian peninsula in the centuries previous to the traditional birth of Jesus Christ (PBUH). Some of these suffering God-men saviors were Osiris, Dionysus, Tammuz, Attis, and Orpheus Bacchus, Mithraism. The Mysteries of Eleusis (initiation ceremonies for the cult of Demeter and Persephone) were also quite popular. (A good sourcebook for further study is The Ancient Mysteries, A Sourcebook for Sacred Texts by Marvin W. Meyer).

The suffering God-man Tammuz, who was worshipped in Syria and earlier by the Sumerians as Dumuzi or Dumizid, is mentioned in the Old Testament in Ezekiel in the eighth chapter. The Prophet Ezekiel (PBUH) is shown "the great abominations that the house of Israel" committed in the Temple. One of these great abominations was that, at the north gate of Jehovah's Temple, sat women weeping for Tammuz. According to this Mystery Religion, Tammuz/Dumuzi was a Sumerian King also known as The Fisherman in some texts and as 'The Shepherd' in others. An ancient text, known as The Courtship of Inana and Dumuzi, tells of a love affair between this King and his wife Inana (Ishtar). The Dumuzi myth states that Dumuzi/Tammuz was killed by demons, but later was brought back to life by Inana. Since Tammuz was the god of Nature and therefore the changing of the seasons, every year some adherents of this mystery religion would "weep for Tammuz," who was present during the seasons when the Earth was alive with vegetation, and absent (dead) during the months when there was not an abundance of vegetation.

The early Church Father Justin Martyr also saw similarities between Christianity and the Mystery Religions. He wrote: "In saying that the Word was born for us without sexual union as Jesus Christ our teacher, we introduce nothing beyond what is said of those called the Sons of Zeus" (Justin Martyr, Apology, 3).

Justin Martyr also stated: "When we say that the Word, who is first born of God, was produced without sexual union, and that he, Jesus Christ, our teacher, was crucified and died, and rose again, and ascended into heaven; we propound nothing different from what you believe regarding those whom you esteem sons of Jupiter (Zeus)" (Justin's First Apology, chapter 21).

These are just two examples of the connection many scholars see between the Ancient Mystery Religions and the Pauline Gospel. Modern Christianity is largely based on the teachings of Paul, who preached the Gospel of "Christ Crucified" (1st Corinthians 2:2). Pauline Christians were initiated into the

Christian Mysteries (1st Corinthians 2:7, 15:51; Colossians 1:26-27, 2:1-3) by baptism (Romans 6:3; Galatians 3:27, Colossians 2:10-15), where the initiates then are given secret wisdom and knowledge (Romans 10:2, 11:33, where wisdom and knowledge are translated from the Greek words Sophia and Gnosis; also: Ephesians 3:4; Colossians 1:9-10, 2:3, 3:10). Paul's "Pastoral" epistles, which many modern scholars believe were written by later Christians against Gnostic Christianity and other perceived heresies, decades after Paul's death, oppose the teachings of the earlier Pauline letters which these scholars consider to be genuine.

THREE

Christianity in the 2nd century of the Common Era.

By the beginning of the 2nd century of the Common (or Christian) Era, there were many sects who called themselves Christians. After the destruction of the Temple in Jerusalem as a result of the First Jewish Revolt against the Roman Empire (66-70 C.E.), the original Jerusalem Christians of Palestinian now had moved to the other side of the Jordan River and lived near the ancient city of Pella. Some of these Jewish Christians tolerated Paul but did not take doctrine from him. Others rejected Paul outright as a false apostle. These sects were known as the Ebionites, Nazoreans, Nazareans, Elchaisites, and Osseans (who may have been the same as the Essenes). They had their own Gospels (which were similar to the canonical Gospels of Matthew and/or Luke). Many looked for leadership from males relatives of Jesus Christ (PBUH), who were called the Desposyni. Some of these Jewish Christians believed the Messiah was the son of two righteous Jews (Joseph and Mary), others believed Mary (PBUH) was a virgin at the birth of Christ. As time went on, these sects were influenced to various degrees by Gnosticism. Some of these groups did not consider Jesus to be a literal son of God, but a human being who was a prophet of God.

The Jewish Christians sects were driven to extinction after Catholic Christianity became the state religion of the Roman Empire. Those that survived east of the Empire were absorbed into Islam in the 7th Century, according to many scholars as diverse as Keith Akers (see "The Lost Religion of Jesus," Chapter 14) and Lutheran pastor and scholar Jeffrey J. Butz (see The Brother of Jesus and the Lost Teachings of Christianity). "The Muslim Jesus: Sayings and Stories in Islamic Literature" by Tarif Khalidi contains sayings of Jesus from Sunni and Shia Islamic sources that present Jesus Christ (PBUH) very similarly to what was seen in classic Jewish Christianity.

Several early Christian sects were influenced by the writings of Paul of Tarsus. They can be divided into three or four main groups – Marcionites, Gnostics, Valentinian Gnostics, and the proto-Orthodox Christians. The Proto–Orthodox would eventually become the Catholic Church, the state Church of the Roman Empire.

Marcion's teachings were based upon his interpretation of 10 of the epistles attributed to Paul of Tarsus. Marcion also used an edited version of the canonical Gospel of Luke. Marcion concluded that Jehovah of the Old Testament was an Evil God, while the Father in the New Testament was the Good God. Marcion's New Testament was the first attempt to choose a New Testament canon.

The Gnostics believed that there were emanations of God which existed in pairs. The Divine Logos was the emanation closest to the source. Sophia (Wisdom) was an emanation who erred and fell by causing the Demiurge to come into being, though Sophia would later be restored. The Demiurge was evil and created the physical universe and humans. The Divine Logos became Christ and preached the secret knowledge to save humans, some of whom had been giving divine essence by the Demiurge. Those humans who had the divine essence would be able to understand the secret knowledge once it was received. Some Gnostics were ascetics, while others were libertine in nature.

The Valentinian Gnostics believed the Demiurge was not evil, but ignorant. The Demiurge (Jehovah) was just but not always good. The Valentinians took a middle way between asceticism and libertinism. They existed within the Proto-Orthodox movement, and Valentinus himself claimed to be a student of Theudas, a disciple of Paul the Apostle. Valentinus had been a candidate for the office of Bishop in Rome, but lost because of his Gnostic views.

The 'Proto-Orthodox' Christians, who would eventually come to be known as the Catholic Church, are known from the writings of Clement of Rome, Justin Martyr, Polycarp, Irenaeus, Tertullian (who first used the Latin word Trinitas to describe the relationship between the Father, Son and Holy Spirit in the late 2nd century) and other 2nd century church fathers. By the end of the 2nd century C.E., all 4 canonical Gospels were accepted by the proto-Orthodox (John's Gospel being the last to be accepted). At least ten of Paul's Epistles were also accepted, as well as the Book of the Acts of the Apostles, the epistles 1st John of 1st Peter. The other canonical books were disputed. The Didache, 1st Clement, and the Shepherd of Hermas held canonical status in many proto-Orthodox Christian centers at the end of the 2nd century, but did not make it into the Catholic New Testament at the end of the 4th century. A few other books that some of these Christians considered to be scripture, such as the Apocalypse of Peter, did not make it into the Catholic New Testament.

FOUR

The Development of the doctrine of the Trinity in the 3rd and 4th centuries C.E.

Various Christian sects within the proto-Orthodox movement were at odds as to how to describe the relationship of the Father, Son and Holy Spirit, and the nature of Christ (PBUH) and the Holy Spirit. A few examples of the various viewpoints follow. Those who followed Cerinthus, for example, believed that Jesus Christ was a human prophet, the Messiah, born to two righteous Jews (as did many of the Ebionite Jewish Christians). The Dynamic Monarchians held that God is one, and the human being Jesus (PBUH) became Christ, the adopted son of God, at his baptism. Some Jewish Christian Gospels as well as early versions of Luke's Gospel have, at Jesus' baptism; where the voice from heaven stated "Behold My beloved son, in whom I am well pleased," quote the Old Testament passage that states "today you have become a son unto me." The Modalistic Monarchians believed that Jesus Christ (PBUH) is the Father, the Son, and the Holy Spirit. Their 3rd century C.E. teacher Sabellius used the phrase "of the same substance" to describe One God who is One Person, who manifests Himself in three modes.

In the mid-to-late 2nd century, those who held similar views to Sabellius were very popular in the local church in the city of Rome. Tertullian and other early Church fathers opposed Sabellius, who was excommunicated as a heretic by Pope Calixtus I in 220 C.E. Tertullian seemed to have taught that the Son was of 'like' substance as the Father, but not the 'same' substance (i.e. the same person as described by the Modalistic Monarchians such as Sabellius).

The Trinity as understood by Tertullian became the popular view among the proto-Orthodox.

Tertullian, it should be noted, had been a Proto-Orthodox Christian. However, Tertullian then became a member of the sect of Montanus. Montanus was a figure of the mid-second century C.E. who taught that he was the promised Comforter, or Paraclete (the spirit of truth) spoken of in the canonical Gospel of John in Chapter 14 (especially verses 16 and 17) and Chapter 16 (especially verses 13 and 14). Montanus was accompanied by two Prophetesses, Priscilla and Maximilla. Anyone who rejected their prophecies and teachings were said to have committed the unforgivable sin. The Montanist sect was most popular in and around the region of Phrygia in Asia Minor. Later then spread to other areas in the Roman Empire and even existed in isolated areas into the 8th Century C.E. Tertullian remained a Montanist until near the end of his life, when he formed his own sect. Because of the strictness of Montanist Christianity and the ecstatic utterances (speaking in tongues) practiced by this sect, some modern scholars compare Montanism with modern Pentecostalism.

Tertullian wrote: "The simple, indeed (I will not call them unwise or unlearned), who always constitute the majority of believers, are startled at the dispensation (of the Three in One), on the very ground that their very Rule of Faith withdraws them from the world's plurality of gods to the one only true God; not understanding that, although He is the one only God, He must yet be believed in with His own economy. The numerical order and distribution of the Trinity, they assume to be a division of the Unity" Tertullian, Against Praxeas, 3. in Alexander Robers and James Donaldson, eds., The Ante-Nicene Fathers (rpt. Grand Rapids: Eerdmans, 1977, III, 598-599).

Later Trinitarians who read the writings of Tertullian see problems in his understanding of the Trinity. While some may see Tertullian as an 'orthodox' writer given at times to clumsy descriptions and explanations, others have seen major problems in his writings. Robert E Roberts, in his book The Theology of Tertullian (published in 1924 C.E. by Epworth Press, Methodist Publishing House) writes in Chapter Six on page 133 that Adolf von Harnack, in his History of Dogma, declares that Tertullian Trinity is purely economic, and (gives as) instances the following defects in his view: " (1) Son and Spirit proceed from the Father solely in view of the work of creation and revelation; (2) Son and Spirit do not possess the entire substance of the Godhead, but, on the contrary, are portione; (3) They are subordinate to the Father; (4) They are, in fact, transitory manifestations; (5) The Father alone is absolutely invisible, and, though the Son is invisible too, He can become visible, and can do things which would be simply unworthy of the Father."

The doctrine of God in Christianity continued to slowly develop (in the writings of Origen of Alexandria and others) until the Arian controversy appeared in the early 4th Century C.E. The Presbyter Arius taught that the Father was eternal, but there was a time when the Son did not exist, nor the Holy Spirit. Thus, Arius taught that the Son was of a different substance than the Father. After Constantine gave Christianity legal standing in the Roman Empire, he called the First Ecumenical Church Council to put an end to the controversies about the nature of God that divided his Christian subjects. At this Council (Nicaea I), Athanasius, then a deacon in the church of Alexandria in Egypt, came up with the formula that became the first part of what was later to be called the Nicene-Constantinopolitan Creed, by stating that the Father and the Son were of the 'same' substance. At the Nicaea I Church Council, the Athanasian Party had the victory and the Arians were deemed heretics. But soon after the council, Constantine learned that the Athanasian Party was also a minority party, and that those who were in the majority still held the view that the Father and Son were of 'like' substance (since the heretic Sabellius used the same language as Athanasius in stating that the Father and Son were of the 'same' substance). Constantine was baptized on his deathbed by the Bishop Eusebius of Caesarea, who wrote the first early history of the Church. Eusebius held the same view of the Trinity as Tertullian and Pope Calixtus I, and thus was called a 'Semi-Arian' by the Athanasians.

After a succession of 'Semi-Arian' Roman Emperors, Julian the Apostate came to the throne. He worked to revive the old Pagan system, but with the charity he saw evidenced by Christianity. After a few years, Julian died. After the reign of a short-lived emperor, Theodosius The Great became emperor. It just so happened that Theodosius was of the Athanasian party. Theodosius soon passed a law that one had to confess the Catholic faith (including the Athanasian formula of the Trinity) to be a citizen of the Roman Empire. Another Church council (Constantinople I) was called in 382 C.E. by Theodosius, which completed the Creed begun at Nicaea I in 325 C.E. Within the Roman Empire, all other Christian sects either died out or were persecuted to extinction (with a few exceptions, such as the Paulicians).

Some non-Trinitarian Christians in the 4th Century C.E. did believe that the Catholic Church (the Proto-Orthodox party) knew there were pagan influences in the doctrine of the Trinity. The 4th Century C.E. Catholic Bishop Marcellus of Ancrya, who was eventually condemned by the Church for teaching a form of Sabellianism, wrote the following: "Now with the heresy of the Ariomaniacs, which has corrupted the Church of God... These then teach three hypostases, just as Valentinus the heresiarch first invented in the book entitled by him 'On the Three Natures.' For he was the first to invent three hypostases and three persons of the Father, Son and Holy Spirit, and he is discovered to have filched this from Hermes and Plato (On the Holy Church, Chapter 9). Marcellus is said to have been present at the Nicaea I council.

FIVE

The final selection of the Catholic New Testament canon at the end of the 4ᵗʰ century C.E.

B eginning with Marcion's early 2ⁿᵈ century collection of 10 letters written by the 'Apostle' (which is how Marcion referred to Paul of Tarsus); there was an attempt by Proto-Orthodox Christians to choose a definitive New Testament Canon. At least 17 or 18 of the 27 books that would eventually comprise the Catholic New Testament Canon were common in Christian centers by the end of the 2ⁿᵈ Century C.E. At the Nicaea I council in 325 C.E., the four canonical Gospels were officially accepted as scripture, while some gospels (such as the Protovangelion of James) were considered to be historical writings by the Catholic Church. By the mid 4ᵗʰ century, the canon was almost closed, except that some Western centers did not accept the Epistle to the Hebrews, while some Eastern centers did not accept The Book of Revelation. In a pastoral letter written about 363 C.E. by Athanasius, who had been a deacon at Nicaea I, but was now the Bishop of Alexandria in Egypt, the 27 books which would become the official New Testament canon were listed. Athanasius also recommended the Didache and the Shepherd of Hermas for private reading. At two North African local church councils (the Council of Hippo in 393 C.E., and the Council of Carthage in 397 C.E.), the New Testament canon was closed for the Western Church. At the Third Ecumenical Council of Ephesus in 430 C.E., the results of the Council of Carthage were accepted by the Catholic Church in the East. A few Eastern centers continued to exclude The Book of Revelation until just before 500 C.E., and do not read from the Book of Revelation to this day in the weekly readings for the Divine Liturgy, although the Book of Revelation is read at other times and in other services.

The Seven Ecumenical Councils of the Church.

From 325 C.E. to 787 C.E., Seven Ecumenical Councils (where the entire Catholic Church was represented) were held to resolve major controversies that had developed in the Church. These seven are listed below:

1. The Council of Nicaea I – 325 C.E.
This council (called by the Roman Empire Constantine) dealt with the controversy over the various views of the nature of God as it pertains to the relationship of the Father and the Son (and the Holy Spirit). The Creed of Nicaea I was produced (using the formula developed by then deacon Athanasius of Alexandria) which stated that the Father and the Son were of the "same" substance (as the Modalistic Monarchians had previously taught), yet the Father and Son were distinct Persons in the Godhead (as the early Trinitarians had taught). Arius, a Presbyter also from Alexandria, who had challenged the definition of the Trinity made by then Bishop Alexander of Alexandria, his boss, was pronounced a heretic for stating The Son was of a 'different' substance than the Father. Those who still held to the early Trinitarian view (that the Father and the Son were of 'like substance') were deemed to be heretics and called 'Semi-Arians.'

2. The Council of Constantinople I – 362-3 C.E.
This council, called by the Emperor Theodosius, added another section to the Creed of Nicaea I by officially declaring that Holy Spirit was also a third Person in the Trinity, and by noting the four marks of the true Church (One, Holy, Catholic, and Apostolic). Although Arianism and the other heresies continued to exist outside the empire, they were now made criminal according to the Roman State.

3. The Council of Ephesus (430-431 C.E.).

This council (called by the Roman Emperor Theodosius II) dealt with the popular theology of the Eastern Christian center Antioch. The Antiochene theology was seen by the Church as teaching that Christ was two persons, the Divine (The Son of God) and the other human (Jesus Christ PBUH the son of Mary PBUH). This doctrine is identified with Nestorius (lived 386-451 C.E.), who was The Patriarch of Constantinople (although he denied holding this belief himself). The Assyrian Church of the East does not teach Nestorianism, but rather that Jesus Christ (PBUH) has 'two gnomes' or essences unmingled and eternally united in one 'parsopa' or personality. Many scholars believe translation problems from Greek into Syriac are the cause of this controversy. As a result of the council, Nestorius was excommunicated, and Antioch lost most of its importance as a major Christian center within the Catholic Church.

4. The Council of Chalcedon (451 C.E.).

This council (called by the Emperor Marcian) dealt with the Eutychian doctrine of Monophysitism. Eutyches, a presbyter of Constantinople, vehemently opposed the doctrine of the Nestorians at the Council of Ephesus. Eutyches went beyond Patriarch Cyril and the Alexandrine school of doctrine by stating that after the union of the two natures (divine and human), Christ had only one nature, the incarnate Word, and thus Christ was essentially different from other humans. It now seems, however, that the problem Eutyches faced was that he could not express his doctrine in a way that safeguarded the two natures in Christ, which the Alexandrine school could do.

The definition of Chalcedon is a creed that teaches that Jesus Christ has two wills and two natures (one divine and one human) and that Jesus Christ (PBUH) is one person, fully Divine and fully human. The result of this council was a major schism. The Coptic Church in Egypt and others Eastern churches considered to have held to Monophysitism are no longer considered heretical, but are now in communion with the Roman Catholic Church.

5. The Council of Constantinople II.

This council, held in 553 C.E., was called by the Byzantine Emperor Justinian I. It also dealt with the Monophysite doctrine. It produced the 'Constitutum' of Pope Vigilius.

6. The Council of Constantinople III.

This council, held in 680-681 C.E., was called by Emperor Constantine IV. It affirmed that the doctrinal conclusion that Jesus Christ (PBUH) had two wills and two natures (human and divine), which did not conflict with or strive against each other. It thus refuted and declared heretical the doctrine of Monothelitism, which, like Monophysitism, held that Jesus Christ had only one divine will. Monothelitism developed under the influence of Patriarch Sergios of Constantinople as an attempt to reconcile Monophysites with the Chalcedonians. A previous attempt to reconcile Monophysites and Chalcedonians, the doctrine of Monoenergism, had failed. The Maronite Church split from the Catholic Church during the time the doctrine of Monoenergism was being developed, but later went back into communion with the Roman Catholic Church and declares that their Christology has always been orthodox. The council condemned Monothelitism.

7. The Council of Nicaea II.
This council, held in 787 C.E., was called by the Empress Irene to restore the honoring of the Icons. Emperor Leo III (717-741) had suppressed the honoring of icons by imperial edict. His son, Emperor Constantine V (741 C.E. – 775 C.E.) had held a synod (called a 'Robber Council' by the Church) to make the suppression of icons official. The veneration of icons was again approved by the Ecumenical Council.

Another controversy not resolved by an Ecumenical Council is the nature of man in relationship to sin. In the very early 4th Century C.E., a British Monk named Pelagius took offence at a prayer written by Augustine of Hippo because Pelagius believed man, as a creation of God, was not weak, nor tainted by the original sin of Adam (PBUH), and therefore could obey God without divine aid (i.e. without God's grace). Augustine, in his "Confessions," wrote about his sins before his repentance toward God and conversion to Christianity. Pelagius, on the other hand, had grown up in a peaceful, Christian household, and even the critics of his teachings, including Augustine, stated that Pelagius was a saintly man. When Pelagianism began to be taught in Rome, its critics became vocal. Augustine drew upon his neo-Platonic philosophical background to oppose Pelagianism. This is when the doctrine of Original Sin was first advanced. Augustine taught that man was unable to please God because of the fall of Adam, since the corruption from the Original Sin is passed on to all of Adam's descendants. Only by the Grace of God (given in the Sacrament of Baptism) can Original Sin be washed away, at which time man is given power to be able to obey God. Then a French Monk named John Cassian entered the controversy. Cassian taught that man is born weak, sick with sin, but by the grace of God can still cooperate with God, even before Baptism. On July 3rd, 529 C.E., the Second Council of Orange, in France, was called and attended by 14 bishops. This council adopted a moderate version of Augustine's views as the doctrine of the Western Church. Pelagianism was condemned as a heresy. Some of John Cassian's books were condemned, but not Cassian himself, who was eventually, canonized a saint. The doctrine of Original Sin would lead to the development of the doctrines of Purgatory, the Limbo of the Lost, and further influence the theology of the Sacrament of Penance. The Eastern Churches accepted the views of John Cassian because, in the view of the Eastern theologians, Cassian's view was more in line with what the proto-orthodox Catholic Church had always taught before the Pelagian controversy. As a result, the Eastern Orthodox today does not hold the doctrines of Purgatory, Limbo, nor the Western view of Penance. This discussion would reappear during and after the Protestant Reformation in the controversy between Calvinism, Arminianism, and Socinianism.

SEVEN

The road to final schism between the Roman and Eastern Orthodox Catholic Churches.

The Catholic Church East and West had differences almost from the very beginning. The Quartodeciman controversy (which excommunicated those Christians who continued celebrating Passover on the same date as the Jews, the equivalent of Nisan 14 on the Julian Calendar) in the 2nd Century C.E., and the battle for supremacy in the Church between the Pope (Patriarch) of Rome and the Patriarch of Constantinople (which was considered New Rome in the East) from the 4th Century C.E. to the Final Schism in 1054 C.E. show how differently the Catholic Church developed on both sides of the Roman Empire. Two important events will be discussed in the following paragraphs in this section.

1. The Council of Constantinople IV.
This council (held in 869-870 C.E.) is considered the 8th of 21 Ecumenical Councils recognized by the Roman Catholic Church. The Eastern Orthodox Church considers Nicaea II to be the final ecumenical council, for the Orthodox Christians only recognize the first seven ecumenical councils. Thus, this is considered to be a Robber Council by Orthodox Christians. The Roman Catholics call the resulting schism, The Schism of Photius, but since the Eastern Orthodox canonized the Patriarch Photius as a saint, they call the resulting schism "The Great Schism."

The Emperor Basil I and Pope Adrian II convoked this council and had papal legates preside over the council. Photius, the Patriarch of Constantinople, was deposed from his seat as a result. One of the main reasons Photius was deposed is because he condemned any additions to the original Nicene-Constantinopolitan Creed, which included the addition of the clause "and the Son" to the Creed after the point where the Creed states "The Holy Spirit, who proceeds from the Father ..." The result of the 1st and 2nd Ecumenical Councils, and reaffirmed at the 3rd Ecumenical Council, Bishops in Spain who were dealing with the remnants of the Arian Christians had inserted the Filioque clause in an attempt to defend the faith. Western pilgrims to Jerusalem offended the Eastern Christians by reciting the Filioque clause. The matter reached the ears of the Patriarch of Constantinople, who complained to the Pope in Rome. The Pope of the time agreed that the Filioque was an illegal insertion. Even Pope Leo III in the Ninth Century C.E. actually had two silver plaques publicly display the Creed written in Greek, without the Filioque clause, as a sign of unity with the East (which resented the new 'Holy' Roman Empire in the West and Charlemagne in particular). In any case, during the reign of Pope Leo III, there was no Creed at all in the Mass celebrated in Rome.

The Patriarch Photius had been installed by the emperor although only a laymen. Photius, in his work "the Mystagogy of the Holy Spirit," had shown philosophically why the Filioque, a development of the theological writings of Augustine of Hippo, had neo-Platonic elements which compromised the Monarchial element of the Trinity. In other words, The Son and Holy Spirit were not merely co-eternal with the Father, but also co-equal with the Father (according to Augustine of Hippo). Further, by stating that the Holy Spirit proceeds from the Son as well as the Father, a new dogma is taught without the authority of an Ecumenical Council of Bishops from the entire Church (East and West).

In 877, Photius was restored as Patriarch of Constantinople by order of the Byzantine Emperor. Many Eastern Orthodox theologians and bishops now consider the reunion council held in Constantinople in 879-880 as possibly being an 8th Ecumenical Council, but the status of Ecumenical is not officially recognized. However, this council did officially restore Photius as Patriarch and excommunicated anyone who altered the original Nicene-Constantinople Creed, thus condemning the Filioque clause.

2. The Great (East-West) Schism of 1054 C.E.
When Cardinal Humbert, the papal legate sent by Pope Leo IX, excommunicated Patriarch Michael I of Constantinople, Michael responded in kind. A mutual excommunication was the result of an extended period of estrangement between the two Patriarchates of Rome and Constantinople. This schism came about mainly because of disputes over papal authority. The Pope

claimed to hold authority over the four Eastern Patriarchates (Constantinople, Alexandria, Antioch, and Jerusalem). The Eastern Patriarchates claimed the primacy of the Papacy was only honorary (i.e. that Rome was the 'first among equals'). Another major reason for the Schism was the addition of the Filioque clause into the Creed. Other less significant controversies that contributed to the Schism concerned differences in liturgical practices and conflicts over jurisdiction. Attempts at reunification were made at the Second Council of Lyons (1274 C.E.) and the Council of Basel (1439 C.E.), but these agreements were never accepted by the majority of Eastern Orthodox Christians. Later attempts have also failed. However, several Eastern Churches (such as the Byzantine Ruthenian Church) have switched allegiances, and are now called Eastern Rite Roman Catholic Churches. The sack of Constantinople by the French armies of the 4th Crusade in 1204 C.E. has also been hard to forget for many traditionally-minded Orthodox Christians. Both the Roman Catholic Church and the Eastern Orthodox Church claim to be the 'One, Holy, Catholic, and Apostolic' Church.

EIGHT

The Crusades (1092 C.E. – 1291 C.E.).

The Crusades were a series of military campaigns or Roman Catholic Holy Wars that were fought during the 11th, 12th, and 13th centuries C.E. Usually, they were called for and supported by the Papacy. Most were attempts to recapture the Holy Land from the Muslims, although some were directed at heretics in Europe. There were 13 major crusades (as numbered by the majority of Western scholars), nine of which were directed toward Muslims in the Middle East.

Although the First Crusade began when Pope Urban II answered the plea of Byzantine emperor Alexius I for help to resist Muslim military campaigns into the Byzantine Empire, the causes for the Crusades were many in number. The conquest of Palestine in the 7th century by the early Islamic state had little effect on Western Christianity, especially since Catholic Pilgrims were allowed to continue their pilgrimages in peace. However, by the 11th century, The Roman Catholic Church leaders saw a chance to advance the fortunes of the Church by calling another Crusade. As Emperor Alexius I would soon find out, the response was much larger and less helpful than the emperor had desired. The Pope not only called for a large army to defend the Byzantine Empire, but also for the capture of Jerusalem. When Jerusalem was captured in 1099, the Crusaders massacred the population (which consisted of Muslims, Jews, and Eastern Orthodox Christians).

Some of the seeds of the Crusades can be seen in earlier events in Europe:

1. Iberian Christians were fighting disunited Moorish emirs and finding some success.

2. Lands traditionally held by the Byzantines, but now in Muslim hands, were being fought for by the maritime states of Pisa, Genoa, and Catalonia.

3. Viking and Magyar lands had been Christianized, which led to a period of fairly stable national boundaries, but also a large population of warriors who knew no other trade.

4. At this same time, the common people of Europe were becoming passionately interested in the controversies within the Church.

5. Because of the Great Schism of 1054 C.E., the Papacy believed that having a Roman Catholic state in the Middle East would give the church an opportunity to dominate the Patriarch of Constantinople.

6. In 1009 C.E., the Fatimid Caliph al-Hakim bi-Amr Allah had the Church of the Holy Sepulcher in Jerusalem destroyed. Although his successor allowed the Byzantines to rebuild the church and to again allow pilgrimages, rumors began to spread of the cruel treatment of Muslims toward pilgrims. These rumors energized the Crusades.

The Crusader Kingdom of Jerusalem existed from 1099 to 1187 C.E., when Saladin recaptured the City of Jerusalem. The Third Crusade was preached by Pope Gregory VIII. Several European leaders, including Philip II of France, Richard I (The Lion-Hearted) of England, and Frederick I, the Holy Roman Emperor, heeded the call. The Crusaders were able to recapture Acre, and defeat the Muslim forces near Arsuf. Though in sight of Jerusalem, the Crusaders (now led by Richard I) were only able to make a truce with Saladin.

The 4th Crusade was called by Pope Innocent III in 1204 C.E. The Venetians were able to persuade the Crusaders to attack Constantinople instead, where they might be able to place a rival Byzantine ruler on the throne. As it turned out, the Byzantine ruler was able to regain the throne without use of the Crusaders. Since they had come all the way to Constantinople to fight, the Crusaders demanded to be paid for their efforts by the Emperor. When the Emperor tried to raise taxes to pay the Crusaders, the citizens rioted. The Crusaders, fearing they would not be paid, sacked the city. The French soldiers went so far as to storm the Church of the Haghia Sophia (Holy Wisdom) and have a prostitute stand on the altar and sing ribald songs. The soldiers destroyed the icons of the Church, and committed sacrileges against the consecrated bread and wine they found on the altar. It is said that when word of this atrocity reached Pope Innocent III, he shuddered. In any event, the leaders of the 4th Crusade were excommunicated, but not before they installed a Latin Patriarch in Constantinople. Many of the Greek Orthodox Christians have never forgiven the Pope or the French for the destruction wrought on the altar of the Church of the Haghia Sophia.

The Albigensian Crusade, which was launched in 1209 C.E. against the 'heretical' Cathars, who flourished in Southern France. Since it was difficult to determine who was a Cathar and who was a Catholic, at times whole populations were destroyed. After some decades, the Cathars were destroyed. Southern France lost its independence in the process.

The 5th Crusade was launched after the Fourth Lateran Council (1215 C.E.) in an attempt to recover the Holy Land by going through Egypt. After a brilliant military victory at Damietta in Egypt in 1219 C.E., the papal delegate Pelagius urged the Crusaders to attack Cairo. That foolish order by the papal delegate, along with the flooding of the Nile, forced the Crusaders to surrender.

The 6th Crusade was launched by the excommunicated Holy Roman Emperor Frederick II in 1228 C.E. He was able to gain Jerusalem, Nazareth, and Bethlehem for the Crusaders for a period of ten years.

The 9th Crusade by the future Edward I of England was launched in 1271 C.E., with very little success. Antioch had already fallen in 1268 C.E. Tripoli would fall in 1289 C.E. and with the fall of Acre in 1291 C.E., the Christian occupation of Syria came to an end.

.

NINE

Extra Ecclesiam Nulla Salus – Outside the Church there is No Salvation.

The Fourth Lateran Council of 1215 C.E. declared the following: "There is indeed one universal church of the faithful, outside of which nobody at all is saved" (Confession of Faith, 1).

The Papal Bull "Unam Sanctum" (The One Holy) was promulgated by Pope Boniface VIII on November 18th 1302. This is considered the strongest statement ever produced by the Roman Catholic Church of the doctrine that outside the Church there is NO Salvation. Some highlights of the Bull follow:

1. "Therefore, of the one and only Church there is one body and one head, not two heads like a monster." Thus, the Pope is stated to be the absolute head and the only head of the Church.

2. "We are informed by the texts of the gospels that in this Church and in its power are two swords; namely, the spiritual and the temporal." Thus, all temporal authorities (such as Emperors and Kings) are subject to the higher spiritual authorities (i.e. the Pope and the Magisterium of the Roman Catholic Church).

3. The Bull concludes with the words, "Furthermore, we declare, we proclaim, we define that it is absolutely necessary for salvation that every human creature be subject to the Roman Pontiff."

Unam Sanctum was issued by Pope Boniface VIII because of a conflict he was having with King Philip IV of Spain, who was attempting to stop the Pope from receiving money from taxes. However, from this Papal Bull and from the declaration from the Confession of Faith of the Fourth Lateran Council, one can see how the Papacy viewed the authority of the Roman Catholic Church:

1. No one may be saved unless they are within the Church.

2. All temporal authorities ought to be subject to the Pope.

The EENS doctrine would have a profound effect upon how the colonization of the New World would take place about two centuries later (when the Pope declared that only the good Roman Catholic countries Spain and Portugal were authorized rule the newly discovered land). This doctrine would also contribute to the Protestant Reformation, the rumblings of which were first heard during the years of the Crusades. The nailing of the 95 Theses (The Disputation of Doctor Martin Luther on the Power and Efficacy of Indulgences) to the door of the Castle Church in Wittenberg by Luther on October 31st, 1517 C.E. was merely the end of the beginning of the Reformation.

TEN

Scholasticism (1100 C.E. – 1500 C.E.).

S cholasticism, from the Latin 'scholasticus' which means 'that which belongs to the school' is the school of philosophy taught in medieval universities from the 12th through the 16th centuries. A work by a highly respected scholar would be studied thoroughly. Word studies and logical analysis were used during the critical examination of the work.

Some of the famous authors and books studied by scholastic philosophers were the Bible, Aristotle and Ibn Rushd (known as the Philosopher and Commentator respectively), Augustine of Hippo, and Plato's book "Timaeus."

Scholastic Philosophy had a major impact on the development of Roman Catholic thought and theology in the 12th through 16th centuries. Some famous Scholastics are Anselm of Canterbury, Pierre Abelard, Peter Lombard, Roger Bacon, Thomas Aquinas, Boethius de Dacia, Duns Scotus, William of Ockham (known for "Ockham's Razor"), and Albertus Magnus. Some well known anti-Scholastics were Bernard of Clairvaux (who was scholasticism's fiercest opponent), Rene Descartes (although his method and terms were influenced by Scholasticism), Thomas Hobbes, and Galileo Galilei. Since it would not be practical to describe the contributions of all these philosophers in this chapter, only the most important philosophers to our discussion, Aquinas and Anselm, will receive short comments below.

1. Anselm of Canterbury (1003? – 1109 C.E.) was a famous medieval philosopher and theologian, and an Archbishop of Canterbury. Anselm is considered the founder of the Scholastic school of Philosophy, and was the inventor of the Ontological Argument for the existence of God. Also, Anselm

was the first Christian theologian to describe the Atonement of Christ as a literal commercial transaction whereby God the Father's honor and holiness, offended by the sin of mankind, is literally paid off as a result of the suffering of Christ. Though not popular in his time, this Commercial Satisfaction view of the Atonement, described in Anselm's book "Cur Deus Homo?" which is Latin for "Why the God-man?," was accepted by the Lutheran and Reformed Protestants during the Reformation, and is believed and taught by most Evangelical Christians into the 21st century C.E. An Appendix below will briefly describe the major theories of the Atonement that have been propagated during the history of Christianity.

2. Thomas Aquinas (c. 1225 C.E. – 1274 C.E.), is considered to be the greatest Roman Catholic philosopher and theologian, and is the father of the Thomistic school of Philosophy. His most famous works are the "Summa Theologiae" (the sum total of Catholic Theology) and the "Summa Contra Gentiles." He completed the development of the Roman Catholic doctrine of Transubstantiation to describe how the bread and wine are changed into the body and blood of Christ during the Mass by using Aristotelian philosophy. Aquinas is also highly respected by Lutheran and Reformed Protestant theologians despite his work on the doctrine of Transubstantiation.

ELEVEN

Important non-Catholic sects from the 5ᵗʰ century to the Protestant Reformation.

From the First Century C.E. to the present, Christianity has never been a monolithic religion. Although the Athanasian Party eventually won out in the 4ᵗʰ century C.E. within the Roman Empire by imperial pressure, and called itself the 'One, Holy, Catholic, and Apostolic' Church which Christ built, within and without the Roman Empire there were still Christian sects who were labeled heretics by their Catholic opponents.

Among the various Palestinian Jewish Christian sects that either tolerated but did not take any doctrine from Paul of Tarsus, or who rejected Paul outright as a false apostle, it appears that the Ebionites (who believed Jesus Christ PBUH was the son of two righteous Jews and who was adopted as a 'son of God' at his baptism) became extinct after the first decade of the 5ᵗʰ century. However, the Nazorenes appear to have existed in some form right up to the advent of Islam in the early 7ᵗʰ century. In fact, the Arabic word for Christian in the Holy Quran is very close to the Hebrew word 'Notzrim,' which in English is 'Nazorean.' More than one Western non-Muslim scholar has speculated that many of the Muslim/Sufi sayings of Jesus Christ (PBUH) came from these Jewish Christian sects which fled Palestine into Western Arabia after the two Jewish Revolts against the Roman Empire in the late 1ˢᵗ and early 2ⁿᵈ Centuries C.E. One may compare the description of the Ebionites given in chapter 30 of the Panarion (or "Medicine Chest") of the early church father Epiphanius of Salamis, volume 1, translated by Frank Williams with "The Ascetic Sayings of Jesus" by Rev. James Robson of Glasgow University, as well as "The Muslim Jesus: Sayings and Stories in Islamic Literature" by Tarif Khalidi.

For a compilation of 12er Shia Muslim traditions attributed to Jesus Christ, see "Jesus Through the Quran and Shia Narrations" by Mahdi Muntazir Qa'im and al-Hajj Muhammad Legenhausen.

Before I list some verses from the Quran concerning Jesus Christ (PBUH) the son of Mary (PBUH) the Virgin, I would like to list some interesting apocryphal Christian traditions. Most of these can be found in The Complete Gospels, edited by Robert J. Miller.

From the fragmentary Gospel of the Hebrews, a non-canonical, somewhat "Gnostic" Gospel used by Jewish Christians, the early church father Origen, writing in the early 3rd Century C.E., preserves this saying of Jesus:

"Even so did my mother, the Holy Spirit, took me by one of my hairs, and carried me to the great mountain Tabor." (Origen, from his Commentary on John 2:12)

About a century later, the church father Epiphanius the Bishop of Salamis wrote about the Gospel of the Hebrews. In his Panarion (or Medicine Chest, where sects considered by Epiphanius are discussed), according to the information he had at the time, which may or may not be accurate, that Jewish Christians of his time also used the Gospel of the Hebrews, which he believed to be the Gospel of Matthew, which these heretical Christians had preserved in the original Hebrew text.

A few decades after Epiphanius wrote his Panarion, the church father Jerome wrote:

"In the Gospel of the Hebrews that the Nazarenes read, it says, 'Even now my mother the Holy Spirit carried me away.' This should upset no one because 'spirit' in Hebrew is feminine, while in our language it is masculine and in Greek it is neuter. In divinity there is no gender." (Jerome, in his Commentary on Isaiah 40.9)

And:

"In the Gospel which the Nazarenes and the Ebionites use which we have recently translated from Hebrew to Greek, and which most people call The Authentic Gospel of Matthew, the man who had the withered hand is described as a mason who begged for help in the following words: 'I was a mason, earning a living with my hands. I beg you, Jesus, restore my health to me, so that I need not beg for my food in shame.' (Jerome, in his Commentary on Matthew 2)

Finally, Cyril of Alexandria, writing in the 4th century C.E., paraphrases a passage from the Gospel of the Hebrews in his Discourse on Mary the Mother of God:

"… when Christ wanted to come to earth, the Good Father summoned a mighty power in the heavens who was called Michael and entrusted Christ to his care. The power came down into the world, and it was called Mary, and Christ was in her womb for seven months. She gave birth to him and he grew up and he chose the apostles who preached him everywhere. He fulfilled the appointed time that was decreed for him. The Jews grew envious of him and came to hate him. They changed the custom of their law and they rose up against him and laid a trap and caught him. They turned him over to the governor, who gave him back to them to crucify. And after they had raised him on the cross, the father took him up to heaven to himself."

What is reported here by Origen, Epiphanius and Jerome and Cyril is important because it demonstrates that Jewish Christians known to them used a Semitic language scripture and reported that Jesus Christ called his mother 'The Holy Spirit.' A later Church Father, Nicephorus, a Patriarch of Constantinople in the early 9th Century C.E., wrote that The Gospel of the Hebrews contained about 2200 lines, just 300 shorter than the canonical Gospel of Matthew. (Ron Cameron, 'The Other Gospels')

One criticism made by conservative western Evangelical Christian scholars of the Quran is that Muhammad (PBUH) did not understand the Trinity because the Quran describes the Trinity as being composed of 'Allah, Jesus, and Mary.' If Muhammad has been born in, say, the 6th Century C.E. in Asia Minor or Gaul or Rome, this would be a legitimate criticism of the Quran. However, Muhammad was born in 6th Century C.E. in the city of Mecca in the Hijaz of the Arabian Peninsula. The Christians (and Jews) that lived in Arabia were not Roman Citizens and did no have to hold to the Catholic faith, nor the Catholic New Testament. Muhammad's revelations in the Quran concerning Christians (and Jews) would be made in the context of Christians sects that existed in late 6th Century C.E. and early 7th Century C.E. Arabia, which would certainly include the Jewish Christian sects (some of whom had Gnostic beliefs) discussed above, and might also include the sect of the Collyridians, who worshipped Mary as a Goddess. The Collyridians are mentioned in the Panarion of Epiphanius, writing in the 4th century C.E.

It is not known if the Collyridians were still in existence at the advent of Islam, or not.

It should be noted that scholars are of differing opinions about how many Jewish Christian non-Canonical gospels were actually in circulation. Some early church writers talk of the Gospel of the Hebrews, while some name the Gospel of the Ebionites and others the Gospel of the Nazarenes. In The Complete Gospels, Robert Miller groups the fragments preserved in the writings of church fathers according to their identification by the church fathers.

Some verses from the Quran concerning Jesus Christ are listed below from Shakir's translation.

1. Known as "Isa Ibn Mariam" or "Jesus the son of Mary."
When the angels said: O Mariam, surely Allah gives you good news with a word from Him (of one) whose name is the Messiah, Isa son of Mariam, worthy of regard in this world and the hereafter and of those who are made near (to Allah) (Quran 3:45).

2. Mary (PBUH) conceived her son (PBUH) while remaining a virgin.
She said: When shall I have a boy and no mortal has yet touched me, nor have I been unchaste? He said: Even so; your Lord says: It is easy to Me; and that We may make him a sign to men and a mercy from Us, and it is a matter which has been decreed. So she conceived him; then withdrew herself with him to a remote place (Quran 19:20-22).

3. Jesus Christ (PBUH) is a prophet and a man, not the literal son of God.
He said: Surely I am a servant of Allah; He has given me the Book and made me a prophet; And He has made me blessed wherever I may be, and He has enjoined on me prayer and poor-rate so long as I live; and dutiful to my mother, and He has not made me insolent, unblessed; And peace on me on the day I was born, and on the day I die, and on the day I am raised to life. Such is Isa, son of Mariam; (this is) the saying of truth about which they dispute. It beseems not Allah that He should take to Himself a son, glory to be Him; when He has decreed a matter He only says to it 'Be,' and it is. And surely Allah is my Lord and your Lord, therefore serve Him; this is the right path (Quran 19:30-36).

4. The enemies of Jesus Christ (PBUH) did not kill him.
And their saying: Surely we have killed the Messiah, Isa son of Mariam, the messenger of Allah; and they did not kill him nor did they crucify him, but

it appeared to them so (like Isa) and most surely those who differ therein are only in a doubt about it; they have no knowledge respecting it, but only follow a conjecture, and they killed him not for sure. Nay! Allah took him up to Himself; and Allah is Mighty, Wise (Quran 4:157-158).

5. Jesus Christ (PBUH) ascended unto God.

And when Allah said: O Isa, I am going to terminate the period of your stay (on earth) and cause you to ascend unto Me and purify you of those who disbelieve and make those who follow you above those who disbelieve to the day of resurrection; then to Me shall be your return, so l will decide between you concerning that in which you differed (Quran 3:55).

6. Do not worship or rely on Jesus Christ (PBUH) as a partner with God.

Surely the likeness of Isa is with Allah as the likeness of Adam; He created him from dust, then said to him, 'Be,' and he was. (This is) the truth from your Lord, so be not of the disputers. But whoever disputes with you in this matter after what has come to you of knowledge, then say: Come let us call our sons and your sons and our women and your women and our near people and your near people, then let us be earnest in prayer, and pray for the curse of Allah on the liars. Most surely this is the true explanation, and there is no god but Allah; and most surely Allah-- He is the Mighty, the Wise. But if they turn back, then surely Allah knows the mischief-makers. Say: O followers of the Book! Come to an equitable proposition between us and you that we shall not serve any but Allah and (that) we shall not associate aught with Him, and (that) some of us shall not take others for lords besides Allah; but if they turn back, then say: Bear witness that we are Muslims (Quran 3:59-64).

Later Jewish Christianity tended to be tinged with Gnostic ideas. Some of these sects came to believe that the Blessed Virgin Mary (PBUH) was the incarnation of the Holy Spirit, and that Jesus Christ (PBUH) was the incarnation of the Divine Logos, both of which were not without beginning, but were emanations from the Godhead. The Collyridians (which were probably a Nestorian sect) had a similar belief. This 'Trinity' is composed of God the Eternal Father, Jesus Christ (PBUH) the Word of God, and the Virgin Mary the Holy Spirit (Greek: Sophia, the Holy Wisdom). Another sect that might be considered a cousin to the Jewish Christian is the Mandaeans of Iraq and Iran. They are sometimes called Sabeans. The Mandaeans accept John the Baptist (PBUH) as the Teacher of Righteousness, but do not consider themselves to be followers of Jesus Christ (PBUH). The Mandaeans are the only Gnostic sect that has survived from the times of the Jewish and Christian Gnostic period. For basic information on the Mandaeans, see "Gnosis: The

Nature and History of Gnosticism" by Kurt Rudolf, and "The Gnostic Bible" by Willis Barnstone and Marvin W. Meyer. Lastly, it should be noted that the 10th century C.E. Karaite scholar Jacob Al-Kirkasani, in History of Jewish Sects, writes of "Yeshua., who the 'Rabbanites' or Rabbis called 'the son of Pandera,'" a Roman soldier, as Jesus the Son of Mary (PBUH), in what seems to be sympathetic terms.

Of the non-Catholic Gentile Christian sects, the Paulicians are a very important group who are first heard from in the middle of the 6th Century C.E., existing in Armenia, and associated with the Nestorians. The Paulicans appear to be influenced by Marcion, and some contemporary opponents wrote that the Paulicians took their name from a heretic named Paul of Samasota, although the Paulicians themselves (and some opponents such as Photius, the Patriarch of Constantinople) state their name is from the Apostle Paul, whom they revered. Like Marcion, the Paulicians held the Gospel of Luke and the Pauline Epistles in high esteem. Most Paulicians held to an 'Adoptionist' Christology (in that they believed Jesus (PBUH) was a human prophet who was adopted as the Son of God at his baptism). They rejected the Sacraments of the Catholic Church, with the exception of Baptism, which the Paulicians considered to be a very important practice. The Paulicians were iconoclasts, and only moderately ascetic. They were sporadically persecuted by the Byzantine Roman Emperors, though a Paulician state existed in Turkey for a time. Persecution by the Byzantine Rulers led the Paulicians to become allies with the Muslims, who never persecuted them. In the 10th Century C.E., those living in Syria were moved by the Byzantine Emperor to the Balkans, where a somewhat similar sect, the Bogomils, existed. Although the remaining Paulicians in Armenia became extinct sometime after the 11th century, the Bogomils became an important sect into the Late Middle Ages.

The Bogomils were a Medieval Gnostic dualist sect that existed in Bulgaria (though with influence elsewhere), where the movement thrived between 10th and 15th centuries C.E. Their doctrine and practice held elements of both the Armenian Paulicians and the Slavonic Church reform movement. The Bogomils were the connecting link between sects in the East and West deemed heretical by the Catholic Church. Their teachings were spread all over Europe. The Cathars were greatly influenced by the Bogomils, and The Cathari Albigensians were actually declared the local versions of the Bogomils in Southern France by the Roman Catholic Church. The Bogomils were Adoptionist, believing that Jesus Christ (PBUH) had human parents and was adopted as a son of God at his baptism by grace, just like other prophets. God, according to Bogomils teachings, had two sons, Sataniel and Michael.

The elder son rebelled against the father and became an evil spirit. After his fall, Sataniel created the lower heavens and the earth, but needed help from his father to create Man. Michael was sent in the form of a man, which the Bogomils identified as Jesus Christ (PBUH) after his baptism. Christ (PBUH) then received power to break the clay tablet (covenant), which was being held back by Sataniel from Adam. After this, Sataniel now became Satan (for he was no longer considered the son of the father, which is the meaning of the "-ail" ending of his former name). Bogomils believed that God, not Jesus Christ (PBUH), would preside over the Judgment. They also were influenced by the Manicheans. Veneration of images and icons were rejected as idolatry. The Orthodox Church was believed to have been set up by Satan after his defeat. The Turks, when they came into possession of lands inhabited by Bogomils, did not persecute them. In fact, the Patarenes (a Bogomil sect) are said to have become Muslims. By 1650 C.E., the Bogomils of Pavlikeni were in decline, and so became Roman Catholics. After this time, beginning in the 18th century C.E., they were persecuted by Turks. About 10,000 Pavlikeni still live in Romania today, while one village exists in Serbia.

The Cathari (probably from the Greek Katharoi, or 'Pure Ones') were a Christian religious movement with Gnostic elements that originated in the middle of the 10th century. The Cathari existed throughout most of Western Europe (from Spain to England and Germany). However, their home was in Southern France, where they were also called Albigensians (from the end of the 12th century). Considered heretics and severely persecuted by the Roman Catholic Church, they have many similarities to the Bogomils and Paulicians. Very little literature has survived from the Cathari, so it is not known with precision exactly what they believed and practiced. It is known that they protested strongly against corruption in the Roman Catholic clergy. The Cathari were composed of the believers and the Perfecti. There may not have been any religious obligations on the believers and the Perfecti, except that they promised to receive the one Cathari sacrament, the Consolamentum or Baptism of the Spirit (which would make them heretics as far as the Church was concerned) before their death. After receiving the Consolamentum, they became Perfecti and lived an extremely ascetic life. The Cathari believed the world was evil (created by an evil deity), which shows the influence of early Christian Gnosticism and Neo-Platonism, as seen in Manichaeanism, and in the beliefs of the Bogomils. The Cathari viewed Jesus Christ (PBUH) in a very similar way as the Modalistic Monarchians did in the early Church. Most Cathari, however, also believed that Jesus (PBUH) appeared as an apparition, since they believed the Good God would not take material (evil) form. This belief, also held by some early Christians, is called 'Docetism.'

All of this was, of course, heresy in the eyes of the Church. Thus, the Cathari were the object of a Crusade over a period of time. The Crusaders, who could not tell the Cathari believers from the other (Catholic) inhabitants of the area, had all the residents slaughtered. Other movements identified by the Church with the Cathari, such as the more orthodox Waldensians and the pantheistic Brethren of the Free Spirit, survived into the 14th and 15th century. By then, the early Protestant sects began to replace or absorb these movements.

The Waldensians, although they claim their church has been around since the time of the Apostles, probably came into existence around 1173 C.E. promoting true poverty, public preaching, and literal interpretation of the Bible. They were declared heretical and so were persecuted by the Roman Catholic Church. A successful merchant known as Peter Waldo (who may or may not have been the source of the name Waldensian) gave away his possessions and became an itinerant preacher, begging for his livelihood. In this way, he shared many views with Francis of Assisi, founder of the Franciscan order in the Roman Catholic Church. However, Peter Waldo preached without permission from the local clergy. While his piety was respected by the Pope, he was asked not to preach without permission from the local clergy. Nonetheless, he continued to preach (even though the clergy would not give him permission to do so). As a result, the Waldensians were declared heretics for 'having contempt for ecclesiastical power,' and the persecution that followed radicalized the sect. The Waldensians were also persecuted for translating the Bible into the language of the local people. Peter Waldo and the Waldensians created a strategy for meeting secretly with Waldensian believers in various towns. A 'Barba' was a traveling preacher who could be a man or a woman, who would travel to various towns and hold meetings where the believers would confess sins and have a worship service. In 1215 C.E. at the Fourth Lateran Council, the Waldensians (along with the Albigensians) were more formally declared heretical. The Waldensians were not Gnostic Dualists like the Cathari, and believed in the Trinity as well. They considered the Pope and his bishops to be murderers because of persecutions and crusades, joining forces with the Protestant Churches a few centuries later. The Waldensians still exist today, although some in the United States have become Presbyterians.

TWELVE

The Seeds of the Protestant Reformation

When Augustinian Monk and Theologian Martin Luther nailed the 95-Theses on the door of the church in Wittenberg, Germany on October 31st 1517 C.E., this event is popularly considered the beginning of the Protestant Reformation. However, for a few centuries previous to this event, others had tried to bring about reform within the Roman Catholic Church. The Waldensians, which were described in the previous section, could have been described in this section also, for they were also somewhat of an influence upon the Reformation. Instead, this section will describe John Wycliffe, the Lollards, and John Hus.

John Wycliffe (c. 1320 C.E. – December 31st 1384 C.E.), is called by many the "Morning Star of the Reformation." He was a philosophy teacher at Oxford who saw Plato, Augustine, William of Ockham, and others as superior to Aristotle (who at the time was popular with many Scholastics Churches). In 1361 Wycliffe became rector of the church at Fillingham. While at Oxford, he was known for his outspoken criticism of the Roman Catholic Church in its attempt to control the government in England. The Church owned much of the wealth in England, which led Wycliffe to call for reforms within the clergy, since he believed the Church should be poor, as in the time of the Apostles. He also believed that the Bible, not the Roman Catholic Church, should be the source of doctrine. At this time in history, the Church only allowed the Bible to be published in Latin, and the few Bibles that existed were owned by the Church, as laymen were not allowed private ownership. Thus, laymen could only receive knowledge from the priest. Wycliffe influenced the Lollards, itinerant preachers in England, as well as a reform movement in Bohemia (where John Hus came upon the writings of Wycliffe and headed a reform movement in his country). The results of Wycliffe's writings caused revolution in Bohemia. The Church condemned Wycliffe and expelled him from Oxford. Forty-four years after Wycliffe died, the Pope ordered his body exhumed and burned.

The Lollards were a political and religious movement in England in the late 14th century. They were influenced by the teachings of John Wycliffe. They believed a priest must be pious in order to perform the sacraments, and in a 'lay priesthood.' They denied the doctrine of Transubstantiation and instead taught Consubstantiation as the view of the real presence of Christ in the Eucharist. The Lollards also taught the concept of the 'Church of the Saved,' which overlapped with but did not include all in the Roman Catholic Church. The name Lollard may come from the Latin word lolium, which means tares or weeds, meaning they were considered to be weeds growing in the 'garden' of the Church. The name might also be a parody of the Lollards teachings that they were the true believers or 'grain' within a weedy Church. One group of Lollards set forth their beliefs before the English parliament in a document called the "The Twelve Conclusions of the Lollards." By the early 15th century, extreme measures by the Church and State sent the Lollards underground. They existed to the beginning of the English Reformation.

John or Jan Hus (c. 1369 C.E. – July 6th 1415 C.E.) of Bohemia was a religious reformer influenced by John Wycliffe, and was condemned as a heretic and excommunicated at 1411. Condemned at the Council of Constance, Hus was burned at the stake. His dear friend, Jerome of Prague, who had introduced Hus to the writings of Wycliffe, was martyred a year after Hus. After the death of John Hus, his followers split into two parties. Sigismund, the Holy Roman Emperor, decided to crack down upon the Hussites. After three anti-Hussite crusades and a Civil War, it is said that the population of Bohemia shrank from 3 million before the wars down to 800,000. Even Joan of Arc wrote a letter to the Hussites stating she would personally lead a crusade against them. The Ultraquist party, which was the moderate party, won out in the end, striking a deal with the Roman Catholic Church. The Taborites, the more radical party, were defeated and formed a group called the Bohemian Brethren, also called the Unity of the Brethren.

In 1620, during the Counter-Reformation within the Holy Roman Empire, those who were outside the Roman Catholic Church were forced to leave their countries or practice underground. Those Brethren who left Bohemia fled to Germany to regroup, and found sanctuary in the lands of Count

Nicholas Ludwig von Zinzendorf. They formed what was initially called in Canada and the USA (except Texas) the Moravian Church, and elsewhere (including Texas) as the Unity of the Brethren, except in the Czech Republic, where they are called Jednota Bratrská.

THIRTEEN

The Protestant Reformation

1. Four Roots of the Protestant Reformation: Historians and Christian scholars usually list four roots of the Protestant Reformation. They are as follows:

i.   Movements which were opposed to the Roman Catholic hierarchical church government. The Cathari and The Waldensians were two examples of such movements.

ii. Schism within the Roman Catholic Church which produced the Avignon Papacy, during which time the Pope was made a captive and lived in Avignon, France. This is often referred to as the 'Babylonian Captivity of the Church.'

iii. The work of early reform leaders such as John Wycliffe (who also made a translation of the Bible that could be read by the common people who had little or no knowledge of Latin) and John Hus, whose followers actually saw a few reforms become reality (in the Czech nation only).

iv. What is called the 'Northern Renaissance,' the spreading of the Renaissance from Italy first to France, then to the Low Countries and Germany, and then finally to England (by the 16th century). One mark of the Northern Renaissance, unlike the Italian Renaissance, was the centralization of political power, which led to the emergence of powerful nation states in Western and Central Europe.

Since a good introduction to the Reformation would only be accomplished by writing an extensive book, I will only touch on the major figures and movements of the Reformation. In addition, there was the Magisterial Reformation which was state-sponsored, and the Radical Reformation, which had no state-sponsorship. Lastly, a major reason the Magisterial Reformation was successful was the threat of Islamic invasion, which led Roman Catholic German Princes to ally (rather than go to war) with Protestant German Princes.

2. Martin Luther (b. November 10th, 1483 – d. February 18th 1546 C.E.) was a Theologian, Augustinian Monk, and church reformer. Initially, Martin Luther followed his father's wishes to go to law school. That all changed, however, when he was nearly hit by a lightning bolt during a thunderstorm, which led him to join the monastery (out of superstition, according to some biographers) in his hometown of Erfurt.

As a young monk, Martin Luther led a very ascetic life and often fasted, whipped himself, spent extra time in prayer, and constantly went to confession. However, the more Luther tried to do for God, the more he became aware of his sins. As a result, his superior had Luther pursue an academic career. Luther was ordained a priest and received a doctorate in theology at the University of Wittenberg, where he was called to the position of 'Doctor in Biblia.'

While earning his doctorate degree, Luther did intensive scripture study. Martin Luther came to believe that the Church had lost sight of the doctrine of grace, and the distinction between Law and Gospel. As can be seen in his commentaries on Romans and Galatians, which were based on his lectures to his student in 1515-1516 C.E., Luther's views on grace and justification differed from the views of the Roman Catholic Church.

While serving both as a professor at Wittenberg and as the preacher at Castle Church (which also served as an Augustinian Monastery), where Luther was a subject of Frederick the Great, Elector of Saxony. During this time, the Dominican Friar Johann Tetzel was selling papal indulgences by using the jingle "as soon as the coin in the coffer rings the soul from purgatory springs." Luther became concerned for the spiritual welfare of his parish because he saw indulgences as an abuse which would lead to neglect of true repentance, and confession. Eventually, on that fateful day at the end of October in 1517, Martin Luther nailed his 95 Theses on the door of the Castle Church as an open invitation to debate the subject of indulgences.

It was not Luther's intention (this early at least) to stir up trouble. The 95 Theses were written in Latin, not German, which was the language of the scholars. It was common to nail invitations to the door of a church to invite scholarly debate. Also, Tetzel was abusing indulgences in the manner in which he advertised them. However, the 95 Theses were translated into German and, with the aid of a relatively new invention called the printing press, the 95 Theses were distributed quickly throughout Germany, and eventually beyond.

It soon became clear that Luther's views were at odds with the Papal Bull "Unigenitus" of Pope Clement VI, issued in 1343 C.E. Because Frederick I did not wish to part with his theologian, and the present Pope, Leo X, wanted Frederick I to be the next Holy Roman Emperor, the pope could do nothing at this time. However, Cardinal Cajetan, considered to be the top Roman Catholic theologian at the time, was dispatched to receive Luther's submission at Augsburg in 1518 C.E. When Martin Luther appeared at Augsburg, he believed he would have a chance to debate the Cardinal. However, Cajetan was only looking for Luther to recant his position. Cajetan slyly maneuvered Luther into denying Unigenitus, and thus papal authority.

Luther was asked to keep silent and write a humble letter to the Pope, along with a paper demonstrating his faithfulness to the Church. Luther agreed to keep silent and write the paper but it was never sent, since it contained no recantation. In July 1519 C.E., Luther had the chance to debate Johann Eck, the leading theologian in Germany, at Carlstadt. Eck managed to get Luther to deny papal authority, with Luther stating that the "power of the keys" was given to the Church, i.e. the congregation of the faithful. Luther spoke of the validity of the Greek Orthodox Church, which was not under Papal authority. Eck claimed afterwards that he was able to get Luther to admit his doctrine was the same as John Hus, an arch-heretic who had been burned at the stake.

Luther's writings were beginning to reach France, England, and Bohemia. Students came to Wittenberg to hear Luther speak. Philip Melancthon joined Luther in teaching duties about this time. Luther's Commentary on Galatians was published, along with other writings which criticized the Church's doctrine of transubstantiation, as well as the Church's views on supererogatory works. In 1520 C.E., three major treatises were written and published by Luther:

1.   To the Christian Nobility of the German Nation,

2.   Prelude to the Babylonian Captivity of the Church, and

3.   On the Freedom of a Christian.

The same year, the Pope warned Luther in the papal bull Exurge Domine that Luther risked excommunication unless he recanted on 41 points within

60 days. Luther responded by sending the Pope his paper on the Freedom of the Christian. John Eck arrived with a Papal ban on September 21ˢᵗ 1520. Luther responded by promptly burning the bull, which upon expiration in 120 days would mean formal excommunication unless Luther recanted. On January 3ʳᵈ, 1521, Luther was excommunicated in the bull Decet Romanum Pontificem.

The ban could not be enforced, however, because Luther was being protected by Elector Frederick III, without hindrance from the new Emperor Charles V.

The Diet of Worms, which had been summoned by Emperor Charles V, opened on January 22ⁿᵈ, 1521 C.E. Luther had been summoned to the Diet to either renounce or reaffirm his views. Johann Eck showed Luther a collection of his controversial writings and asked Luther if he still believed what was written in these books. When Luther requested time to think about the matter, the time was granted. Luther prayed and sought counsel from his friends. The next day at the Diet, Counselor Eck asked, "Would Luther reject his books and the errors they contain?" Luther's response was: "Unless I am convicted by Scripture and plain reason, I do not accept the authority of popes and councils, for they have contradicted each other; my conscience is captive to the Word of God. I cannot and will not recant anything, for to go against conscience is neither right nor safe." It is said that Luther finished by declaring, "Here I stand. I can do no other. God help me. Amen."

Luther left Worms to return to Wittenberg before the Diet reached a decision about what to do about Luther. The Elector Frederick had Luther arrested before he reached Wittenberg. Finally, the Emperor issued the Edict of Worms on May 25ᵗʰ, 1521 C.E. The Edict declared Luther a heretic and an outlaw. His writings were banned. Meanwhile, Luther was taken captive by allies and held prisoner for about a year in Castle Wartburg at Eisenach. During this time, Luther made his famous German translation of the New Testament (published 1522 C.E.). Many Saxon clergy were actively putting Luther's writings into practice, which caused much commotion. The Anabaptists from Zwickau were much more radical than Luther in their reforms, and so Luther secretly returned to Wittenberg to preach, which put a stop to the Anabaptist work there. Luther would also side with the Elector against the Peasants revolt of 1524-25 C.E., which was a response in part to his writings and the writings of the Anabaptists. Luther's "Against the Murderous, Thieving Hordes of the Peasants," published in 1525 C.E., called for a swift and bloody punishment of the peasants. Luther recognized and taught obedience to secular authority, yet many considered Luther's words a betrayal.

Concerning the Bible, Luther had a low view of the Old Testament book of Esther, as well as the New Testament books of Hebrews, Jude, James, and Revelation (not unlike some earlier Church Fathers), even going so far as to refer to the Book of James as an "Epistle of Straw." Yet, Luther never removed them from the New Testament. His translation of the Old Testament, based upon the Hebrew Masoretic Texts rather than the Greek Septuagint, was published in 1525 C.E. That same year, Luther married a former nun, Katharina von Bora, with whom he fathered six children (3 boys and 3 girls).

At the Diet of Augsburg in 1530 C.E., convened by Emperor Charles V to stop the growing Protestant movement (this included by this time the followers of Luther, the Anabaptists, the followers of Zwingli, and other new groups). Philip Melancthon (considered more diplomatic than Luther) presented a written summary of Lutheran beliefs called the Augsburg Confession. German Princes (and at a later time rulers from other countries) signed the Augsburg Confession as Lutheran territories. The Schmalkald League was organized by these German Princes in 1531 C.E. As a result, the Schmalkald War was fought by these princes against the armies of the Emperor Charles V. The Emperor then tried to force Roman Catholicism again on those lands which he conquered, but this action did not destroy the Lutheran movement. Luther himself died in Eisleben, the city of his birth, in 1546 C.E.

Luther considered The Bondage of the Will and the Small Catechism (written along with the Large Catechism in 1528 C.E. at the request of the Elector Frederick) as his best works. Others would include his commentary on Paul's Epistle to the Galatians in this list. Luther is also still remembered for his book "On the Jews and Their Lies," which was written in his later years. Luther initially believed the Jews would respond to the Gospel as taught by Luther and his fellow workers. But after several years, the Jews did not respond, and so Luther became very critical of the Jews. Also, Luther was intolerant of the beliefs of other Protestant Reformers (Calvin, Zwingli, the Anabaptists, and etc.) even if the differences in doctrine were few.

After the deaths of Luther and Melancthon, Lutheranism became divided into factions, one adhering strictly to the writings of Luther, and the other holding views held by Melancthon. In 1577, a group of Lutheran theologians headed by Martin Chemnitz, and based on previous work by Jacob Andrae and others, defined a doctrinal statement to unite these factions. Titled the Formula of Concord, it was included in a volume called The Confessions of the Lutheran Church, and popularly known as the Book of Concord. The Book of Concord, which is still used by almost every Lutheran denomination today, contains The Augsburg Confession, the Apology to the Augsburg Confession, and the Treatise on the Powers and Primacy of the Pope, all written by Melancthon, as well as Luther's Large and Small Catechisms, and his Schmalkald Articles, and the Formula of Concord. The largest Protestant sect in Christianity is the Lutheran denominations. One out of every five Protestants is a Lutheran and one out of every twenty Christians is a Lutheran.

I will only write one or two paragraphs for those Protestants…

3. John Calvin (b. July 10, 1509 C.E. – d. May 27th, 1564 C.E.) is the French Theologian from whom Calvinism derives its name. He received a Doctor of Law degree at Orleans. After fleeing France because of his Protestant views, he was persuaded to come to Geneva by the reformer William Farel in 1536 C.E. Calvin was pastor of the church in Strasbourg from 1538 to 1541 C.E., and then returned to Geneva, where he lived until his death in 1564 C.E. Although Calvin's greatest work by far was his Institutes of the Christian Religion (which is still widely used in the 21st century), he also wrote commentaries on the books of the Bible. Influenced heavily by Augustine of Hippo (as was Luther), Calvin's writings spread throughout much of Europe, and Calvinism was brought from England to North America by the Puritans, as well as by the Dutch.

When Calvin returned to Geneva, he helped to set up in this city a theocratic rule, including a consistory which dealt minor penalties to those who taught false doctrine, or those who publicly displayed a lewd lifestyle. In 1553 C.E., Calvin approved of the burning at the stake of Michael Servetus for the heresy of denying the Trinity (although Servetus believed in the deity of Christ in the same was as the Modalistic Monarchians). Calvin also opposed the medieval Roman Catholic ban on usury, though he did state that poor people in dire need should be loaned money without charging interest.

4. William Tyndale (b. 1484 – d. 1536 C.E.) was a priest and scholar who translated the Bible into English not long after the invention of the printing press in Europe. The King James translation is mainly based upon the translation made by Tyndale. Tyndale accepted the doctrines of the Protestant Reformation, which were considered heretical by the Roman Catholic Church and initially by the Church of England. He met with early leaders of the English Reformation. Tyndale's Bible translation was banned by the Church of England, which led the martyrdom of Tyndale (who was burned at the stake) by agents of King Henry VII in 1536 C.E. Tyndale's last words were "Lord, open the King of England's eyes!"

5. Thomas Cranmer (b. July 2, 1489 – d. 1556 C.E.) was an important English reformer during the reigns of King Henry VIII and his son King Edward VI. Cranmer was the Archbishop of Canterbury from 1533 C.E. until just before his death. Cranmer became an important figure after the death of Henry VIII because he was able to advise Edward VI, who wanted to reform the Church of England (which had broken with the Roman Catholic Church when Henry VIII was unable to obtain an annulment of his first marriage from the Roman Catholic Church, yet did not reform the English Church except to close the monasteries). In 1549 C.E., Cranmer introduced the first Book of Common Prayer, the first complete official book of Anglican Church worship. When Queen Mary I succeeded Edward VI upon his death in 1553 C.E., she desired to once again to have England be a Roman Catholic nation. Cranmer recanted Protestantism to avoid the wrath of Mary, but eventually Cranmer was removed from office, imprisoned, and charged with both treason and heresy in February 1556 C.E. Mary had personal reasons to oppose Cranmer, which included his annulment of her parents marriage (leaving her an illegitimate child) and his signing (under pressure from her brother King Edward VI) to change the law of succession to allow Lady Jane Grey to become Queen of England, though she reigned only 9 days, rather than Mary. When Cranmer learned that he was to be burned at the stake, he withdrew his recantation of the Protestant Faith. It is said that at his execution, Cranmer thrust the hand that signed the recantation of Protestantism into the hottest part of the fire, saying the hand that signed the recantation should burn first.

6. Ulrich Zwingli (b. January 1st 1484 – d. October 11th, 1531 C.E.) was a Roman Catholic priest and leader in the Swiss Reformation and the founder of the Swiss Reformed Churches, and was independent from Martin Luther. Supported by the government and people of Zurich, Zwingli's movement was known for persecuting Anabaptists and others. Zwingli met Luther at Marburg, Germany, in 1529 C.E. They had significant differences in their sacramental views. Zwingli as a priest had a 'clerical marriage,' a common concubinal arrangement at the time, with Anna Reinhard. They formally married in 1534 C.E. and had four children. Switzerland had no real central government at the time, and so a civil war developed between Roman Catholic districts and reformed districts. Zwingli fell in battle on 1531 C.E. in a surprise attack by Roman Catholic soldiers on Zurich, for Zwingli marched out with the first of the soldiers. The army of Zurich was defeated in Kappel, which was followed by a peace treaty there a little more than a month later. Zwingli was succeeded by the well-known reformer Heinrich Bullinger.

7. **Zacharias Ursinus** (1534 C.E. – 1583 C.E.) and Caspar Olevianus (1536 C.E. – 1587 C.E.) are German Reformed theologians best known for composing the Heidelberg Catechism used by German and Dutch Reformed churches. The Heidelberg Catechism was the most popular non-Lutheran Reformed Catechism during the Reformation, and is still used today by many Reformed churches. Several teachers of the period of the Protestant Reformation recommended the Heidelberg Catechism be read first before delving into John Calvin's Institutes of the Christian Religion. The Synod of Heidelberg approved the catechism in 1563 C.E. Since the catechism was divided into 52 sections, one could teach from a section every Sunday of the year. In the Netherlands in the 16th Century C.E., The Heidelberg Catechism was approved by several synods, along with the Belgic Confession and the Canons of Dordtrecht as the Three Forms of Unity of the Dutch Reformed Churches.

8. **The Anabaptist** (re-baptizer) Movement was a major wing of the Radical Reformation, despite having no magisterial support, and came into existence in the early 16th Century C.E., although the Waldensians, Brethren of the Common Life, and even the Hussites may be considered their forerunners. The name comes from the practice of baptizing only adult believers. Although some early Anabaptists used military means (such as the Munster Rebellion – 1532 C.E. – 1535 C.E.), those which survived to the present time have been pacifistic churches. The Amish, Hutterites, and the Mennonites are present-day examples of this movement. The Baptists claim to have emerged out of this movement in the early 17th century. The Dordrecht Confession of Faith (1632 C.E.) gives a good outline of early Anabaptist beliefs, especially those of Menno Simons, from whom the Mennonites receive their name.

Besides the Mennonites, some other existing Anabaptist groups include the Amish, the Hutterites, the German Baptists (or Dunkards), and the Brethren in Christ. All of these groups are known as Peace Churches, although some of the Brethren groups in modern times have not stressed non-violence as a distinctive practice.

A favorite book of Mennonites is the Martyrs Mirror. First published in 1660 in the Dutch language by Thieleman J. van Braght, the Martyrs Mirror is a history of Christian Martyrs who were killed for their faith by the Roman Empire, as well as Catholic and Protestant State churches from the first century to 1660. The Hutterite Chronicle is a similar book written by Hutterite Anabaptists.

9. The Socinians were Radical Reformers who followed the teachings of Laelius Socinus (died 1562 C.E. in Zurich, Switzerland) and Faustus Socinus (died 1604 C.E. in Poland). These Reformers rejected the doctrine of the Trinity and Divinity of Jesus doctrine. They believed that the State should allow religious freedom. Their views are summarized in The Racovian Catechism, which was published in 1605 C.E. There was a major community in Rakow, Poland, which was broken up by their persecutors in 1643 C.E. The Socinians influenced biblical Unitarians in Europe, and later in New England.

10. A summary of important Protestant Reformers not mentioned above would include names such as:

   i.   Savonarola (born September 21st 1452 C.E. – died in Florence, Italy on May 23rd 1498 C.E.), who was a Dominican priest, and briefly, ruler of Florence. He preached against the Renaissance and morally lax living. In 1497, he carried out the Bonfire of the Vanities, where he had boys go house to house collecting luxury items which were to be destroyed. On becoming sole ruler of Florence (after defeating Lorenzo de Medici, a former patron), he changed the penalty for committing sodomy from a fine to a capital offense. In 1497 C.E., he was condemned as a heretic by Pope Julius II. The following year, Savonarola was hanged and burned at the same time.

   ii. Martin Bucer (1491 C.E. – 1551 C.E.) was a German Reformer with Zwinglian Theological views. At odds with the Lutherans, he was invited to England by Archbishop Cranmer to teach, and was consulted on the revision of the Book of Common Prayer. He died in 1551 C.E. In 1557 C.E., Queen Mary, a Roman Catholic, had his body dug up and burnt. His grave was restored by Queen Elizabeth I when she restored the Church of England.

   iii. Heinrich Bullinger (1505 C.E. – 1575 C.E.) was a Swiss Reformer, who, although not as controversial as Luther or Calvin, was a major influence on the Reformation. After the Battle of Kappell (1531 C.E.) where Zwingli was defeated, Bullinger moved to Zurich and it is said his preaching led some to remark that he was "Zwingli resurrected like a phoenix." Later that year, he replaced Zwingli as the leader of the Zurich church until his death in 1575 C.E. Bullinger is the author of the "second Helvetic Confession," and important Reformed Confession of Faith. The late 19th Century C.E. bible scholar E. W. Bullinger is one of his descendants.

iv. Frederick III, Elector Palatine of the Rhine (born February 14th 1515 C.E. – October 26th 1576 C.E.) must be mentioned as an important figure of the Reformation. He inherited his title from the Elector Otto-Henry, Elector of the Palatine, in 1559 C.E., after Otto-Henry failed to produce an heir. Frederick III was a devout Calvinist convert who made Calvinism the official religion of his lands, allowing Reformed Calvinism to thrive within the Holy Roman Empire. The Heidelberg Catechism is said to have been written under his supervision.

v. John Knox (born either in 1513 or 1514 C.E. – d. 1572 C.E.) was a Scottish Reformer who helped lead the reforms in Scotland in a Presbyterian manner. Knox became a Protestant in 1546 C.E., and after a period of confinement, was on the continent from 1554 C.E. – 1559 C.E., spending time in Geneva, Switzerland. Returning to Scotland in 1560, Knox played in leading role in organizing the Church of Scotland after the Roman Catholic Church was voted out as the state religion by parliament.

11. The Five "Solas" of the Protestant Reformation emphasize the view of the Magisterial Reformationists that Christ, not the Papacy, was the head of the Church. The Five Solas are listed below in Latin and English:

i. Sola Gratia – By Grace Alone

ii. Sola Fide – Through Faith Alone

iii. Solus Christus – Christ Alone (or sometimes: Solo Christo – By Christ Alone)

iv. Sola Scriptura – The Bible Alone

v. Soli Deo Gloria – Glory to God Alone

FOURTEEN

The Roman Catholic Counter-Reformation (sometimes called the Restoration).

The Roman Catholic Counter-Reformation, which climaxed in the Council of Trent (the 19th of 21 Ecumenical Councils of the Roman Catholic Church), was partly a reaction to the Protestant Reformation. However, the Church also sought to reform from within. There is also a political aspect to the Counter-Reformation, especially concerning the nation of Spain and particularly with regard to the reign of King Philip II.

1. There were reforms made within in the Church itself. Parish priests became better educated. Rural priests were given more opportunities for theological education. Church administration was improved by combating "absentee-ism," whereby a Bishop neglected to visit and supervise outlying parishes. Piety and recitation of the Rosary was encouraged, and an attempt was made to improve public morality.

2. New religious orders came into being at this time. Among these orders were the Jesuits (founded by Spanish nobleman Ignatius Loyola (1491 C.E. – 1556 C.E.), and the Capuchin, an offshoot of the Franciscans. These orders contributed to the improvement of morality and piety of the parishes. The orders also helped to stem corruption within the church. Founded in 1534 C.E., the highly educated Jesuits helped to curb the spread of the Reformation in various European countries. The evangelical practices of the Jesuits even outpaced the aggressive efforts of the Calvinists.

3. The Council of Trent, which met in three sessions between 1545 C.E. and 1563 C.E., was called by Pope Paul III, whose pontificate last from

1534 C.E. to 1549 C.E. The Council made several institutional reforms to curb corruption and abuses, but affirmed the doctrines and practices of the medieval Roman Catholic Church. The Council reaffirmed salvation by faith and works, and the authority of the Papacy and Church Tradition; as well as the doctrines of Transubstantiation, the Seven Sacraments, the Cult of Saints and Relics, Pilgrimages and Indulgences, and Mariology. Doctrines of the Protestant Reformers were condemned as heresies.

4. The fortunes of Spain were to have a positive impact on the Counter-Reformation. The Reconquista had successfully allowed Spain to reclaim Iberia, by forcing the Muslims and the Jews to leave Spain. Roman Catholic Spain was able to successfully colonize the Americas and elsewhere, including the Philippines Islands, named after King Philip II. Thus, the Spanish were able to spread the Church throughout the world.

5. The fall of Constantinople to the Turkish Caliphate deserves mention, because the fall of the Greek Roman Empire (called the Byzantine Empire in the West) left several Orthodox jurisdictions without any protection. For instance, Orthodox Christians in Eastern Europe could no longer look to Constantinople for protection, so jurisdictions such as the Ruthenian Orthodox became "Byzantine Catholics," looking to the Papacy for leadership, yet keeping their liturgy and practices. The Uniate Churches, literally 'Eastern Churches United with Rome,' are nowadays called 'Eastern Catholics.'

FIFTEEN

Christianity in the 17th Century C.E.

After the Protestant Reformation of the 16th Century C.E., more Christian sects came into being in Europe. This, of course, meant more controversies and more wars. In this chapter we will touch on a few of the important developments within Christianity that took place in the 17th Century C.E.

1. The Remonstrants were Dutch Protestants who followed and developed the teachings of Jacob (or James) Arminius (b. 1560 C.E. – d. 1609 C.E.). Arminius was a Dutch Reformed theologian who eventually came to disagree with the Calvinists on some points of doctrine.

What has become known as Calvinism can be briefly (though somewhat confusingly) described by the acronym TULIP as follows:

T = Total Depravity of Man
U = Unconditional Election
L = Limited Atonement
I = Irresistible Grace
P = Perseverance of the Saints

In a nutshell, a better summary of the TULIP system is the following:

T = Due to the original sin of Adam, humanity is unable to please God and therefore must be punished for the sins that are committed due to man's fallen nature because they are unable to repent and return to God.

U = Before the Creation and subsequent fall of man, God foreknew that man would fall, and therefore God elected some people for salvation by His Grace. Those who were not elected to salvation will be punished for their sins. God is not obligated to save all mankind, since God never ordained that man should sin in the first place.

L = Christ suffered and died for the Elect alone, not for every human being.

I = The Grace of God, which is necessary for salvation, cannot be resisted. Only the Elect is granted this grace and by this grace will have faith in Christ and be regenerated and forgiven of all their sins.

P = The Saints, the Elect predestined by God before the creation, will persevere to the end and be saved. If they backslide, they always repent of their sins and return to their Lord.

The Dutch Theologian Jacob Arminius, who did hold the Heidelberg Catechism and Calvin's Institutes of the Christian religion in high regard, disagreed with some of the points in the acronym TULIP. Arminius agreed with the Calvinists that man was totally unable to please God as a result of the Fall of Adam and therefore was lost without the Grace of God. Arminius also believed that only the Elect of God would be saved. However, Arminius believed that Christ died for all mankind, although only those who actually responded to the grace of God were actually reconciled to God and saved. Arminius believed that God's grace could be resisted, and therefore while Arminius believed the Elect would persevere to the end, Arminius believed someone once saved by grace through faith could reject that salvation and turn away from God.

Arminius complained that many who criticized his conclusions did not accurately represent his teachings, for some compared Arminius to the Pelagians. Arminius never taught that man could be saved apart from the Grace of God, nor did Arminius deny original sin. Arminius was just as much opposed to Pelagian teachings as Calvin was. Arminius died before his followers made their Remonstrance.

In 1610 C.E., the Remonstrants propagated their views in Holland and Friesland, outlining five points of departure from the stricter Calvinists. Although individual Arminians went beyond the actual teachings of Arminius, most of the Arminians of the Remonstrance were in agreement with the views of Arminius. At the Synod of Dordtrecht (1618-1619 C.E.), twelve Arminian pastors headed by Simon Episcopus were defeated. Ninety-three canons were drawn up against the Remonstrants, some of whom were banished. The state did not see the Remonstrants as dangerous, and so Arminian party had some liberty by 1621, and could worship freely anywhere in Holland by

1630. Although they were defeated, the Remonstrants would have a definite influence on Evangelical Christianity.

2. The Baptist churches began to appear in the early 17th Century C.E. John Smyth (b. 1570 C.E. – d. 1612 C.E.), is considered by many historians to have formed the first Baptist church in 1609. Smyth had been ordained an Anglican priest in 1594, but shortly thereafter, Smyth left the Church of England and became a Separatist (called a Non-Conformist by the Anglican Church). Smyth came to reject infant baptism, believing instead in the believer's baptism taught by the Anabaptists. Smyth baptized himself and others, but later rejected this baptism and sought baptism by the Mennonite Anabaptists.

This incident caused a break between Smyth and a group led by Thomas Helwys, whose churches were called General Baptists because they believed the atonement of Christ (PBUH) was not for the elect in particular, but for all of humanity in general. The General Baptists, as a result, held Arminian views.

By the middle of the 17th century C.E., some Calvinists in England began to believe in the doctrine of believer's baptism, and these formed the first Particular Baptist churches, because Calvinists believe that the atonement of Christ (PBUH) was made for the elect in particular, rather than for all humanity in general, as did the General Baptists. Although outnumbered by the General Baptists originally, the Particular Baptists soon overtook the General Baptists in numbers. The First London Confession, published in 1646 C.E. and the Second London Confession, published in 1689 C.E. (although created in 1677 C.E.), are the two most important Particular Baptist Confessions of Faith.

An acrostic using the word Baptist which summarizes popular Baptist beliefs is as follows:

B - Biblical Authority
A - Autonomy of the local church
P - Priesthood of all believers (i.e. no priesthood and laity)
T - Two ordinances (baptism and communion)
I - Individual Soul Liberty (the right to choose one's belief according to conscience)
S - Separation of Church and State
T - Two officers of the church (pastor and deacon)

Various kinds of Baptists denominations and fellowships would come into existence over time (some examples being Seventh Day Baptists, Primitive Baptists, and Reformed Baptists). Even groups who do not use the name Baptist would come to hold many or all of their beliefs.

Landmarkism is a view among some Baptists that developed in 19th Century C.E. America which attempts to trace the existence of Baptists to the time before the Catholic State Church in the 4th Century C.E., all the way back to John the Baptist (PBUH) and Jesus Christ (PBUH). Those Baptists who hold this view believe Baptists are outside of the Protestant Reformation, since the Baptists are a restoration of pre-Catholic Christianity. J. M. Carroll's book "The Trail of Blood," written in 1931 C.E., presents various groups persecuted by the Catholic Church, such as the Montanists, Donatists, Paulicians, Albigensians, Waldensians, and Anabaptists as the succession of Baptist churches, despite the fact that most of these sects held only a few positions similar to Baptists. Not all American Baptists, of course, hold to this view of history.

The name Baptist comes from the Greek word "baptizo," which means "to submerge." This is very close to the Islamic practice of "Ghusl," ritual cleansing by taking a bath in water.

3. The Puritans were English Protestants who sought reforms, and in some cases, even separation, from the Anglican Church, beginning in the 16th Century C.E. and continuing into the 18th century C.E. or even longer. They did not believe the reforms of the Anglican Church under Queen Elizabeth I (who succeeded her Catholic sister Queen 'Bloody' Mary) went far enough. Most Puritans wanted and worked toward either a Presbyterian or Congregationalist form of Church Government rather than the Episcopal form used in the Anglican Church. The early leaders had left England during the persecutions during the reign of Queen Mary, and had been influenced by the Continental Protestants, especially those in Geneva, Switzerland.

The Geneva Bible, which was the English translation of choice by the Puritans, was translated in Geneva. This translation was more popular than the official Bishop's translation of the Anglican Church that followed. When King James I (b. 1566 C.E. – d. 1625 C.E.) came to power and authorized the translation that bears his name, it took the King James Translation about 50 years to unseat the Geneva translation as the favored among the Puritans, and this despite the fact that many of the translators who worked on the King James Bible were Puritans themselves.

Tracts such as the Martin Marprelate made satire of the government and the Anglican Church hierarchy. In the 1570's C.E., Queen Elizabeth I commissioned Richard Hooker to produce a response against the Puritan Presbyterians. Hooker wrote "Of the Laws of Ecclesiastical Polity," which is one of the most important works used by the 'High Church' Anglicans. When Charles I (b. 1600 C.E. – d. 1649 C.E.) succeeded James I as King of England, he was a High Churchmen who backed a sacramental and Arminian theology. Charles I appointed William Laud (b. 1573 C.E. – d. 1645 C.E.) as Archbishop of Canterbury in 1633 C.E. Archbishop Laud was a patriotic Englishman and Anglican Churchman, but was accused of Popery by the Puritans. Laud demanded uniformity within the Church of England including the liturgy and vestments, which was seen by the Presbyterian Puritans as persecution. Laud pushed for this uniformity in the Church of Scotland also, which led to the Bishop's Wars. King Charles asked parliament for funds to fight the First Bishops War in 1639 C.E., but the Presbyterian majority refused, which forced Charles to settle for a truce with the Church of Scotland. More disputes after the truce led Charles to call parliament again in 1640 C.E., but this 'Short Parliament' only lasted a month. After the Second Bishops War ended later the same year with a humiliating loss and the Treaty of Ripon, Charles eventually called the 'Long Parliament.' The Long Parliament forced King Charles into granting various concessions, including the execution of his advisor William Wentworth, and Archbishop Laud.

These events and others in the struggle between King Charles Royalist Party and Parliament eventually led to the English Civil War, which lasted from 1642 C.E. through 1651 C.E., ending with a Parliamentary Victory at the Battle of Worchester. King Charles was beheaded before the end of the war, in 1649 C.E.

Oliver Cromwell (1599 C.E. – 1658 C.E.), who was also known as 'Old Ironsides,' and who had defeated King Charles I with the New Model Army (also called the Roundheads), became Lord Protector of England, Scotland, and Ireland after the defeat of the British Monarchy. His rule lasted from December 1653 C.E. until his death, which may have been from malaria, or from poisoning. Cromwell, a Puritan and a General Baptist, was very anti-Roman Catholic, but at the same time opposed to the more radical Protestant groups in Britain at the time. Cromwell held the view of Divine Providence whereby God was actively directing events in the world, through the actions of the Elect. Cromwell believed he was one of those elect. Although Cromwell did not want to execute King Charles, who believed in the 'Divine Right of Kings,' Cromwell eventually came under pressure from his own army officers to do so. Between 1649 C.E. and 1653 C.E., England was a republic known as the Commonwealth of England, although Cromwell actually ruled as a military dictator. The unanimous support he enjoyed when at war with King Charles came to an end with the King's execution, as infighting broke out among the factions who had supported Cromwell. This led Cromwell to dismiss the 'Rump Parliament' and assume absolute control of the government as Lord Protector. Religious Freedom (including Jews, but excepting for Roman Catholics) was insisted upon by Cromwell.

After Oliver Cromwell's death, his son Richard Cromwell became Lord Protector, but within two years Parliament restored the monarchy, bringing in Charles II as King, because Richard had been such an unworthy successor. In 1661, Oliver Cromwell's body was exhumed and he was executed posthumously, on the anniversary of the date on which Charles I was executed. Cromwell's body was hanged, drawn, quartered, and his body thrown into a pit. His head was stuck on a post outside Westminster Abbey until 1665.

Wars between Roman Catholic and Protestants were not uncommon during this period. The wars in France against the Protestant Huguenots were another example of religious infighting between Protestants and Roman Catholics in this period.

4. The Voyage of the Mayflower, bringing Puritans to what would later be the state of Massachusetts is another important event of the 17th Century C.E. Puritans from England had fled to Holland because of the Reformed Church which existed in that country. However, when these English parents saw that their children were become more Dutch, some decided to set up a colony in the New World. The Mayflower left England in 1620 C.E. and landed at what would be called the Plymouth Colony in August 1621 C.E. The Mayflower Compact was signed November 21st 1621. Since the Pilgrims, as these Puritans were called, had landed outside the chartered land of the London Company, the Compact was created to establish civil government and to show their allegiance to the King of England. Americans celebrate Thanksgiving Day in late November every year as a result of the success of the Plymouth Colony.

5. The Religious Society of Friends, commonly known by the name "Quakers," began in 17th Century England as a group of Christian dissenters who were dissatisfied with existing denominations and sects. This denomination is one of the historic Peace Churches. George Fox (1624 C.E. – January 13th, 1691 C.E.), who was born into a Puritan family, was a serious Christian since childhood. Fox came to look down upon those who professed to be believers in Christ, because of their behavior. Fox heard an inner voice saying, "Thou seest how young people go together into vanity, and old people into the earth; thou must forsake all, young and old, keep out of all, and be as a stranger unto all." Thus, Fox stressed the importance of the "Inner Light" of the Spirit. Fox also believed that since the Bible taught that the Prophets were shepherds or farmers, a preacher of the Gospel did not have to be a graduate of a University and should not be paid. Although persecuted and imprisoned for his preaching during his journeys which began at the beginning of the English Civil War (as recorded in his Journal), Fox came to be respected even by the Lord Protector, Oliver Cromwell. Other early Quakers include Margaret Fell (who married George Fox after her first husband died), James Naylor, Robert Barclay, Isaac Penington, George Whitehead, and William Penn who led the American colony that became known as Pennsylvania (Penn's Forest). Named after Penn's father Admiral William Penn, Pennsylvania was meant to be a colony where religious dissenters could live in peace. The original vision for the Pennsylvania colony was to allow religious freedom for all monotheists (Trinitarian and non-Trinitarian Christians, Deists, Jews, and Muslims), only restricting atheists and polytheists. Benjamin Franklin was influenced by the early Quakers on the view of religious freedom. The Pennsylvania colony came to allow all beliefs and influenced the constitution of the United States.

Some of the distinct beliefs of George Fox are listed below:

i.   Rituals may be ignored as long as one experiences a true conversion by the Spirit of God. Ministerial Qualifications (as noted earlier) are the result of the gifts of the Holy Spirit rather than Seminary study. Thus, even women and children can be ministers of the Gospel.

ii.   Fox called churches "steeplehouses" because he believed God dwells in the hearts of His people, and thus would not be limited to a church building. Fox believed Christians could hold services anywhere, not just in a building with a steeple.

iii. Although Fox supported his teachings using the scripture, he believed that spiritually awakened believers could follow their own inner guide (i.e. their own heart) rather than rely on scripture readings or the sermons are given by paid clergyman. The Quakers practiced "Unprogrammed Worship" where a meeting began in silence and those present would meditate until one was led by the Spirit to pray or give a short exhortation.

iv.   Fox made no clear distinction of the Father, Son and Holy Spirit because the word Trinity is nowhere mentioned in the Bible.

The Quakers encountered controversies and experienced Church Splits in the 1800s and as a result, the three main groups of Quakers in the 21st Century C.E. are:

i.   The Conservative Quakers.

ii. The Evangelical Quakers (who were influenced by the preaching and doctrine of John Wesley).

iii. The Liberal Quakers (some of whom are not Christians, and some of whom are atheists and Polytheists).

This is a short list of books on the early Quakers:

i.   The Journal of George Fox

ii. An Apology For the True Christian Divinity by Robert Barclay

iii. Twenty-First Century Penn – A compilation of some of William Penn's important writings.

SIXTEEN

Some Developments within Anglo-American Christianity in the 18th century C.E.

1. The First Great Awakening, a period of the revival of religion in Colonial America (and to some degree in the UK), occurred in the 1730's and 1740's C.E. Jonathan Edwards sermon "Sinners in the Hands of an Angry God," which was not his original title, is considered to have been the beginning of the period. Edwards, a Calvinist preacher from Massachusetts who intended to revive the spirit of the Puritan pilgrims, was a very powerful speaker and could draw large crowds. The movement continued under the preaching of the English preacher George Whitfield, one of the founders of the Methodist movement although a Calvinist. Whitfield traveled across Colonial America, preaching in a very lively and dramatic manner.

During this period, various itinerant preachers appeared, some having the 'new light' (i.e. using the methods of popularized by Edwards and Whitfield), while others had the 'old light' (i.e. those who gave more of an intellectual discourse without drama or liveliness). Despite the 'old light/new light' controversy, Americans became more passionate about their religious beliefs and began to study the Bible at home. This would contribute to aspects of American culture, such as the rugged-individualism and self-determinism seen in American pioneer stock. The decline that had been seen in American religion as a result of the Enlightenment in European philosophy, and because of the Salem Witch Trials, was reversed for several decades. This was also the last time that Puritan and Calvinist thought would dominate American religion.

2. Methodism is a movement that began in England, within the Anglican Church, by a small group of students at Oxford, who met from 1729 C.E. to 1735 C.E. These students took a methodical approach to Bible study and Christian living, and so were called Methodists by their critics. Among the early Methodists were John and Charles Wesley and George Whitfield. Because the sermons preached were very lively, the movement was accused of fanaticism. The Anglican Church was also concerned about the new teachings of the 'New Birth' and 'Justification by Faith,' as well as the work of the Holy Spirit in the believer's life, which were taught by the Methodists. Eventually, John Wesley became influenced by the Moravians, and also by the teachings of Jacob Arminius. George Whitfield, on the other hand, became a Calvinist and the two had a parting of ways. Calvinist Methodists still exist today, predominately in Wales.

After the American Revolution, The Church of England broke ties with its American counterparts. Wesley sent fellow priest Thomas Coke to superintend the American Methodists. However, since Wesley was only a priest, he did not have the power to ordain a bishop or superintendent. Thus, Methodists broke away from the Anglican Church. John Wesley, however, died a faithful Anglican priest. Francis Asbury, ordained by Thomas Coke, was the first American Methodist Bishop.

3. Universalism, the belief that God does not condemn unrepentant sinners to an eternal hellfire, but eventually saves all people, began to spread in New England during the 18th century C.E. Universalists would use the Satisfaction/Literal Commercial Transaction theory of the Atonement, which states that Jesus Christ (PBUH) paid the sinner's debt to God for offending Him, but unlike the Calvinists, who taught that the benefits of the atonement was only applied to the account of the Elect alone, the Universalists taught that the Atonement was made for all men (on the basis of Bible passages such as 2nd Peter 3:9). Next, Universalists would quote New Testament verses which state that Jesus Christ (PBUH) died for the sins of the whole world. Lastly, they would declare that since Jesus Christ (PBUH) paid in full the debt of the sinner, and since the New Testament states Jesus Christ came to save the World, everyone was going to be saved, and therefore the Revival movements and Evangelical meetings were completely unnecessary.

By 1785 C.E., the Universalist movement had grown large. Therefore, Dr. Jonathan Edwards Jr., the son of the great Revivalist, preached three important sermons, influenced by the writings of Arminius's student Hugo Grotius, which taught that the atonement satisfied public justice, rather than retributive justice as in the Commercial Satisfaction theory introduced by

Anselm and later developed by the Protestant Reformers. Thus, God is willing to forgive repentant sinners, but must satisfy public justice by demonstrating that sin ought to be punished. The Governmental Satisfaction view goes on to state that Christ's atonement is a substitute for the penalty incurred by breaking God's Moral Government. The Commercial Satisfaction theory had stated that Christ's Atonement was a substituted penalty, rather than a substitute for the penalty.

The preaching of the younger Jonathan Edwards did tend to slow the growth of the Universalist movement. The New England/New School theologians continued to teach this view until after the Civil War. Some Wesleyan Arminian theologians began to teach this view also.

Universalists founded their own denomination in 1793 C.E., and later merged with some Unitarians who also held Universalist views. There continued to exist Unitarians who were not Universalists, and some of these Unitarians would influence new American and English religious movements in the next century.

SEVENTEEN

A glance at Anglo-American Christianity during the 19th Century C.E.

In 1776 C.E., the Thirteen Colonies on the North-American seaboard declared independence from the British Empire and become the United States of America. The Constitution of the USA allows for freedom of religion and no 'state' church, which was a fairly new development in the West. As a result, many new Christian Religious Movements appeared not only in the USA, but also in England, which had, over the centuries, become tolerant of religious movements that did not conform to the state Church of England. Some of these important movements were:

- The Cumberland Presbyterians
- New School Evangelicals
- The 7th Day Adventists
- The Mormons
- The Disciples of Christ
- Christian Science
- The Watchtower (Bible Students)
- The Christadelphians and the Abrahamic Faith movements
- The Latter-Rain Movement
- Landmark Baptists
- Dispensationalism

Within the Roman Catholic Church there was the Paulist Fathers order, and the Vatican I Ecumenical Council. Also, events such as the American Civil War, the Downgrade Controversy and the rise of German Higher Criticism, had an effect on Anglo-American Christianity. God willing, some information about these movements and developments will be given in this section.

1. The Second Great Awakening began in 1800 C.E. when a revival began in the Cumberland River Valley in Tennessee. Turning away from the traditional Presbyterian Calvinist doctrine of Predestination, the "Whosoever Will" gospel was preached. By 1810 C.E., various church leaders founded the Cumberland Presbyterian Church, made up partly of those who had left traditional Presbyterian Churches. In later years, some members returned to larger Presbyterian denominations. Cumberland Presbyterians still exist as a denomination in the early 21st Century C.E., along with some smaller churches that trace their history back to the main body. The early Cumberland Presbyterians would hold some doctrines in common with 'New School' Presbyterians during the revivals of the early-mid 1800's C.E. in the United Stated.

2. Dispensationalism, a system of doctrine that is extremely popular in the United States among the majority of Evangelical Christians, was developed by the Irish-English Plymouth Brethren separatist sect in general, and former Anglican Priest Dr. John Nelson Darby (b. 1800 C.E. – d. 1880 C.E.), in the 1820's C.E. The Plymouth Brethren were anti-clerical, anti-denominational, and anti-creedal, in reaction to the Church of England. Darby developed a theological system with new and unique ideas concerning Biblical history and the prophecies concerning the Second Coming of Christ, stating the Christ's return would be in two stages, with the Tribulation period in between these stages. Darby added Dispensationalism to the Futurism of a fellow member of the Plymouth Brethren named George Irving (who had been influenced by a book published in 1812 C.E. by a Jesuit named Manuel De Lacunza, under the pseudonym Juan Josafa Rabbi Ben Ezra). Some scholars even believe Darby's views influenced Britain to make the Balfour Declaration in 1917 C.E.

Dispensationalism, in seeking to work out differences in Old Testament and New Testament theology, postulates that Biblical History can be divided into seven periods or dispensations. The Seven Dispensations are listed below:

    i.   The Dispensation of Innocence (before the fall of Adam) – Genesis 1:1 to 3:7.

ii. The Dispensation of Conscience (from Adam to Noah) – Genesis 3:8 to 8:22.

iii. The Dispensation of Government (from Noah to Abraham) – Genesis 9:1 to 11:32).

iv. The Dispensation of Patriarchs (from Abraham to Moses) – Genesis 12:1 to Exodus 19:25).

v. The Dispensation of the Mosaic Law/Torah (from Moses to Christ) – Exodus 10:1 to Acts 2:4.

vi. The Dispensation of Grace (The current Church Age) – Acts 2:4 to Revelation 20:3.

vii. The Dispensation of the Millennium (literally 1,000 years long) that will soon come– Revelation 20:4 to Revelation 20:6.

Also, Dispensationalism maintains these four tenets:

i. A radical distinction between Israel and the Church as two people of God with different destinies, earthy Israel and the Heavenly Church.

ii. A radical distinction between the Law of Moses and the Grace of God, which are two mutually exclusive ideas.

iii. The New Testament church is a parenthesis in time in God's plan that was not foreseen in the Old Testament.

iv. A distinction between the Rapture and the Second Coming of Christ, where the Rapture of the Church is Christ's coming 'in the air' (1st Thessalonians 4:17) precedes the official Second Coming by seven years, a time known as the Tribulation Period.

As a result, many Dispensationalists refer to Covenantalism, the view of the majority of Protestant Christians previous to the 1880's C.E., as Replacement Theology or Secessionism, since Reformed Covenantalism views Israel as the Old Testament Church, which can now be saved only by accepting the Messiah, Jesus Christ (PBUH), and join the New Testament Church. Some Dispensationalists have even accused Covenantalists of Anti-Semitism. Dispensationalists have consistently followed the teaching of John Darby that the Jews will always be God's Chosen People.

Most Dispensationalists believe the Church Age began with the events chronicled Chapter 2 or the Book of Acts in the Bible. Hyper-Dispensationalists (also known as Ultra-Dispensationalism) believe the Church Age begins later than this. Some believe the Church Age began with the Apostle Paul in the middle of the Books of Acts. Others believe the Church Age begins with the last chapter of the Book of Acts (chapter 28).

Dispensationalism began to spread in the United States as a result of the Niagara Bible Conferences held between 1883 C.E. and 1887 C.E. The American evangelist Dwight L. Moody (1837 C.E. – 1889 C.E.) became sympathetic to Dispensationalist teachings, which began to be taught at the Moody Bible Institute (1886 C.E.) and other new Bible colleges around the country. The Niagara Bible Conferences is also considered the beginning of the modern Christian Fundamentalist movement in the USA.

Cyrus I. Scofield (1843 C.E. – 1921 C.E.), a follower of evangelist D. L. Moody, was ordained as a Congregationalist minister in 1883 C.E. after becoming interested in religion while serving a short jail sentence for forgery in 1879 C.E. Scofield wrote a book called "Rightly Dividing the Word of God." That book was written during the time of the Niagara Bible Conferences, and was based on the writings of John Darby. Scofield, who had no formal ministerial training, put together the Scofield Reference Bible, which was published in 1909 C.E. by the Oxford University Press. As one of the first study bibles to appear, the Scofield Reference Bible popularized Dispensationalism. The 1917 C.E. edition was the best-selling study bible among Fundamentalist Christians for 50 years, helping Dispensationalism replace the Reformed/Calvinist evangelicalism that had been popular previously. The Scofield Reference Bible is considered the intellectual foundation for Christian Zionism in the USA. Hal Lindsey (born 1929 C.E.) published a best-selling book called "The Late Great Planet Earth" in 1970 C.E. which is based upon the timeline of events presented in the Scofield Study Bible. Beginning in 1995 C.E., Dispensationalist author Tim LaHaye (born 1926 C.E.) published the first volume of what would become known as the "Left Behind" series, which is fiction based on the timeline of the Seven-year Tribulation period as described in the Scofield Reference Bible.

There have been attempts in recent decades to improve upon the Dispensationalism of Darby and Scofield. Also, in recent years Covenant Theology has been regaining some of the ground lost to Dispensationalism.

3. Landmarkism is a movement that began within Southern Baptist Convention in the USA in the mid-1800s C.E. Most of the Baptist churches which held their beliefs broke from the Southern Baptists over a period of time. These Baptists tended to be Particular (i.e. Calvinist) Baptists, but later, many Dispensationalist and Fundamentalist Baptists began to hold these same views. Primitive Baptists (another movement of Calvinist Baptists) hold views similar to Landmarker Baptists.

The distinctive teachings of Landmarkism are:

i. The church is local and visible only (in contrast to the view of the visible and invisible church). Only professing Christians in good standing in a local church body have a say in the governing of the local church.

ii. Baptist churches have existed in perpetuity since being founded by Jesus Christ (PBUH) before Pentecost until the modern times.

iii. The Great Commission (in Matthew 28 to "Go therefore to all nations…") was given to the church (i.e. local churches only).

iv. Baptism and the Lord's Supper are church ordinances (not sacraments) that are only valid when administered by a New Testament (i.e. Baptist) Church.

The term 'Landmark' originally comes from two scriptures:

i. Proverbs 22:28 "…remove not the ancient landmark, which thy fathers have set…"

ii. Proverbs 23:18 "…remove not the old landmark; and enter not into the fields of the fatherless…"

J. M. Pendleton first used the term 'Landmark' in a series of four articles written in the Tennessee Baptist, a paper edited by J. R. Graves. Pendleton's articles eventually appeared in a pamphlet titled "An Old Landmark Re-set," which was published in 1856 C.E. This was in response to practices by many members of the Southern Baptist convention, who associated with churches who baptized infants, and who held open communion, i.e. sharing the Lord's Supper with non-Baptists. The Landmark Baptists considered those Baptists who maintained these practices to be liberal. Eventually, the practice of Secondary Separation developed, whereby one local church would break fellowship with another local church because of the liberal practices of the pastor and congregation.

This controversy continued into the 20th century C.E. In 1932, a popular pamphlet appeared called "The Trail of Blood," written by Dr. J. M. Carroll (b. 1858 C.E. – d. 1931 C.E.). The two subtitles, "Following the Christians down through the Centuries… or, the History of Baptist Churches from the time of Christ, Their Founder, to the Present Day," were based on passages in the Bible, "… Overcame Satan by the blood of the Lamb, and by the word of their testimony: and they loved not their lives unto death," from Revelation 12:11. The Trail of Blood lists various Christian sects throughout history which were considered heretical by the Roman Catholic Church, and includes a chart with a timeline listing the approximate dates of the various persecutions, which are indicated in the timeline by a red dot. Critics have complained that Landmark Baptists trace their lineage through various unrelated Christian sects, many of whom (such as the Cathari/Albigensians) would be considered heretical by the Landmark Baptists themselves. Some of these critics are Baptists who do not accept the Landmark position.

4. The Stone-Campbell Restoration Movement, which eventually produced the Christian Church (Disciples of Christ), was an American religious movement in the early 1800s C.E., at the time known as the Second Great Awakening. This movement, which began among Presbyterians, was an attempt to restore what was seen as the New Testament by ignoring what had traditionally accepted in Catholic and Protestant Creeds, which were seen to divide rather than unite Christians. This movement intended to concentrate on the essential elements of Christianity in such a way as to allow diversity in non-essentials. Lay persons administrated weekly the Lord's Supper. The movement practiced believer's baptism by immersion. The movement eventually branched into five denominations, including the Disciples of Christ, the Church of Christ, and the International Church of Christ (or Boston Church of Christ). Also, the early Mormon leader Sidney Rigdon, as well as the founder of the Christadelphians, Englishman Dr. John Thomas, spent time in the movement in its early days.

5. The Adventist Movement, out of which eventually formed the Seventh Day Adventist denomination, was a movement within existing denominations. William Miller (b. 1782 C.E. – d. 1849 C.E.) was an American Baptist preacher from upstate New York. By 1830 C.E., he reached some conclusions about the Second Coming of Jesus Christ (PBUH) and the building of the Temple in Jerusalem. In summary, Miller believed:

i.   In prophetic writings, one day always represents one year.

ii.   The 70 weeks of Daniel 9:24 and the 2300 days of Daniel 8:14 began at the same year.

iii. In viewing history based on Bishop Ussher's chronology, the 70 weeks began in the year 457 B.C.E.

iv.   When referring to the cleansing of the sanctuary in the temple in Jerusalem, Daniel 8:14 is speaking prophetically of Christ's return to earth.

Based on these calculations, the Second Coming of Christ and the start of Millennial Kingdom would begin sometime in the year 1843 C.E. This is why the movement was called the Adventist Movement, because Miller began preaching the Second Advent or Coming of Christ in 1843. Critics of the movement referred to Adventists as Millerites. However, the movement did introduce Millennialism to American Christians, although this form was Covenantal as opposed to Dispensational Millennialism.

Miller soon adjusted his calculations in regards to the Jewish calendar, and became confident that 1844 C.E. would be the time of the Second Coming. Since Miller used Ussher's chronology, which states that the world was created in 4004 B.C.E., and since Miller believed a day was equal to 1000 years in prophecy (based on his interpretation of 2nd Peter 3:8), the Second Coming would be the start of the Seventh Day of Creation. Perhaps as many as 100,000 Adventists were awaiting the Blessed Hope, which Miller believed would come on October 22, 1844. Many had abandoned or sold their farms in expectation of the Blessed Hope.

The failure of the Blessed Hope to appear led to what has been called the Great Disappointment. A very humbled Miller wrote in his memoirs, "Were I to live my life over again, with the same evidence that I then had, to be honest with God and man, I should have to do as I have done. I confess my error, and acknowledge my disappointment." Miller then left the Adventist movement, which now numbered less than 100 men and women.

6. The Seventh Day Adventists, which developed out of the Adventist Movement after the Great Disappointment in 1844 C.E., existed for about 2 decades as a small movement, but became a formally organized church in Battle Creek, Michigan, in 1863 C.E. The leaders had been James White, Ellen C. White (who claimed to be a Prophetess) and Joseph Bates. In the meantime, a Seventh Day Baptist woman named Rachel Oakes introduced the concept of the Seventh Day Sabbath rather than the Lord's Day (i.e. Sunday) as the day of rest and worship. Also, further study of the bible had led to the view that Christ, in the Heavenly Sanctuary, had actually moved into the Holy of Holies to begin his Investigative Judgment in 1844. Other doctrinal developments include the view that when a person dies, he has no conscious existence, and that those judged wicked after the Resurrection will be thrown into the Lake of Fire where they will be annihilated, with no eternal suffering. Like the Baptists, Seventh Day Adventists believe in Believer's Baptism. They also follow the food laws of the Torah, recommend vegetarianism, and discourage alcohol and tobacco use. All of this is done for the health benefits, not to be Torah Observant.

There has been much discussion about the fact that many early Seventh Day Adventists held to a somewhat similar doctrine of God as did Arius in the early 4th century C.E. Jesus Christ (PBUH) was not considered to be the eternal Son of God, the Second Person of the Trinity, but rather the incarnation of the Archangel Michael, and therefore not to be worshipped. While modern Seventh Day Adventists are Trinitarians and teach that Ellen C. White was a Trinitarian also, critics, as well as Restorationist Seventh Day Adventists believe the Prophetess was actually of the non-Trinitarian camp. While some modern Evangelical Christians believe 7th Day Adventists can be true Christians, others do not. Several of the doctrinal developments of the Seventh Day Adventists would influence other unorthodox Christian Movements, such as the Watchtower (Bible Students) led by Charles Taze Russell, the later Watchtower (Jehovah's Witnesses), the Worldwide Church of God founded by Herbert W. Armstrong, and other groups.

7. The Christadelphians and the Abrahamic Faith movements began at the same time, and the important leaders had connections with each other, and also with the Adventist movement and Stone-Campbell Restoration Movement. Dr. John Thomas (b. 1805 C.E. – d. 1871 C.E.), an Englishmen, had a close association with Dr. Alexander Campbell, but because of differences of opinion, Thomas broke from Campbell in the late 1840's C.E. At this same time (1848-49 C.E.), Thomas wrote the book "Elpis Israel," which laid out the basic doctrines of what would become the Christadelphians. Thomas was not a Trinitarian; he believed that Jesus Christ (PBUH) was not co-eternal with the Father, and that the Holy Spirit was not a divine being. He also believed that the dead have no conscious existence until the Resurrection, when the true believers will be raised from the dead to live on earth, which has been restored and can be called paradise. Thomas also believed there was no literal Satan, but that Satan is the tendency in every man to sin. Only believers should be baptized by immersion, and the Lord's Supper was celebrated weekly. Thomas believed his views were the same as the 1st Century C.E. church, from which Christianity had gone astray. Israel, according to John Thomas, would be re-established and Christ would rule from Jerusalem as the Messiah of the Jews, who would be restored to their land.

Another leader with similar views as Thomas was Benjamin Wilson, who was a Greek Scholar and produced a Greek-English interlinear New Testament known as the Emphatic Diaglot. Wilson was not a Trinitarian, and so his interlinear eventually came to be used by many non-Trinitarian groups, especially the Jehovah's Witnesses. A third leader of the time was Joseph

Marsh, who wrote the book Age to Come, which was an alternative view of the Second Coming and the New Earth than what was taught by Adventists.

These three men worked together for a time, but eventually parted ways over controversies. Since the local churches that sprang from the movement were independent churches, the parting of ways led to some confusion. The Christadelphians were the most united group. Other groups of local churches were known by names like Church of God, Faith of Abraham or Church of God of the Blessed Hope or Church of God, Abrahamic Faith. The group that rejected the view that Satan is not a real being came to be called Church of God, General Conference.

Another group which fits somewhere between the Church of God, Abrahamic Faith and Adventists is the Church of God, Seventh Day. They rejected Ellen C. White as a Prophetess, but kept the Sabbath, and they believed in the Abrahamic Faith. The Church of God, Seventh Day, still exists today in two very small conferences.

8. The New School Evangelicalism of the Second Great Awakening was an outgrowth of the theology that was developed in New England by the theological, and indeed physical, descendants of Jonathan Edwards, who is still considered the foremost American theologian. His son, Dr. Jonathan Edwards Junior, had used the Governmental Satisfaction view of the atonement developed by Hugo Grotius, a student of James Arminius, to halt the advance of Universalism in New England. Dr. Timothy Dwight, the son-in-law of the senior Edwards, was also a respected theologian. The New Haven Theologians developed the theology further, until it reached its fullest development under Dr. Nathaniel W. Taylor of Yale, and finally the revivalist Charles Grandison Finney (b. 1792 C.E. – d. 1875 C.E.) who was a successful revivalist, and beginning in the early 1840s C.E., became an instructor at Oberlin College in Ohio. Finney had no college training, but was a leader in the community and an apprentice lawyer. After a dramatic conversion experience, Finney was ordained a Presbyterian Minister at age 29 (though he would later join the Congregationalists). Finney's logical and clear presentation of the Gospel (from the New School point of view) led to the conversion of an estimated 500,000 from his personal appearances as a traveling evangelist. The publication of his book "Lectures on the Revival of Religion," in 1835 C.E., led to similar movements elsewhere in the USA and England. Finney also supported the Abolitionist Movement and would withhold communion from slave owners who attended services where Finney presided.

Finney's methods were criticized by Calvinists, and Finney's Systematic Theology was given a negative review by one of the greatest defenders of historical Calvinism in the 19th Century C.E., Dr. Charles Hodge (1797 C.E. – 1878 C.E.) of Princeton Theological Seminary. Hodge saw utilitarianism and Pelagian views in Finney's writings. Finney responded in the 1851 edition of his Systematic Theology, but Hodge never answered his response.

Another important New School theologian was Albert Barnes (1798 C.E. – 1870 C.E.) who is known for his famous Commentary on the Bible. Barnes was a graduate of Princeton Theological Seminary. He had been tried (but not convicted) of heresy by the more conservative (i.e. Calvinist) wing of his Presbyterian denomination. This trial only served to widen the breach between the New School and the Old School Presbyterians.

The New School movement eventually went into decline for several reasons. After the American Civil War, the New School Presbyterians found that they had become more conservative, and so they eventually re-united with the Old School. Also, beginning about 1880, students who had gone to Europe to study at the prestigious colleges on the Continent began to receive teaching positions in American seminaries. These students brought with them the contemporary philosophical ideas, as well as the German Higher Criticism that attacked the integrity of the Bible. At Princeton, the Calvinists took the lead against those scholars who had brought back the new ideas from Europe. However, about 5 years after the death of Charles Finney, Oberlin College succumbed to the liberal theologians. Andover College, another Congregationalist college, suffered the same fate.

The appearance of the liberal theologians in the 1880s C.E. would eventually lead to the Fundamentalist movement at the beginning of the 20th Century C.E.

9. The Mormons are followers of Joseph Smith Jr., who claimed to be a prophet of God who was directed by the Angel Moroni to find and translate Gold Plates in order to produce The Book of Mormon. Hence the name Mormon applied to Smith's followers. The Book of Mormon is the story of various groups who migrated to the Americas from Asia, and later, from the Holy Land before the Babylonian Captivity of the Kingdom of Judah. Several chapters report that Jesus Christ (PBUH) appeared to the descendants of these people in North America after his resurrection.

Joseph Smith officially formed a church as the Church of Jesus Christ in upstate New York in 1830 C.E., he moved to Kirtland, Ohio to avoid persecution, then to Missouri and Illinois. Sidney Rigdon, who had been a Baptist preacher and later a follower of Alexander Campbell, converted to the Mormon movement and became one of its leaders. Eventually, Joseph Smith Jr. was arrested and eventually murdered by a mob that attacked the jail at Carthage, Illinois. The bulk of American Christians believed then and still believes now that Joseph Smith was a false prophet; the Book of Mormon a false scripture, and opposed the practice of polygamy that began to appear after the Mormons migrated from New York. The Book of Mormon condemns polygamy, but the Mormons also obeyed direct prophecies given by Joseph Smith, some of which support the practice.

The Mormons considered themselves a Restoration movement, and their prophet Joseph Smith Jr. was seen as one actually restoring the original Christianity which had been corrupted by the Roman Catholic Church, and unsuccessfully reformed by the Protestants. Many non-Mormon writers, as well as a Mormon group who follows the teachings of the late Jack Raveill (who may have been a member of the Mormon splinter group Church of Christ, Temple Lot), have demonstrated using the Book of Mormon that Joseph Smith originally held to a form of the Modalistic Monarchian view of the Oneness of God (i.e. that Jesus Christ (PBUH) was actually God (the Father) in the flesh, yet as a human person prayed to God the Father as the Divine Person. Later, Joseph Smith's teachings on the nature of God and other subjects changed, as can be seen when comparing the original Book of Commandments of 1833 with the first Doctrine and Covenants edition of 1835, which contain revelation Joseph Smith claimed he received from God. Polygamy, Baptism for the Dead, and many other doctrines and practices were among the new teachings that would be taught by Smith (or perhaps by his close associates).

After the murder of Joseph Smith in 1844 C.E., the Church of Jesus Christ, as the Mormons referred to their church, became fractured. The majority followed Brigham Young to Deseret, the area now known as Utah. They founded Salt Lake City and several other cities and towns. Converts from Northern Europe came to Salt Lake City. The practice of polygamy reached its full measure in Utah, but because of pressure from the United States government, the practice was officially abandoned by the main Utah group, who referred to their church as The Church of Jesus Christ of Latter-Day Saints. As a result, in the 20th century, several groups of fundamentalist sects led by a 'prophet' sprang up in Utah continuing the practice of polygamy.

Meanwhile, various Mormon churches formed among those who had rejected Brigham Young as their leader. The largest church was the Reorganized

Church of Jesus Christ of Latter-Day Saints or RLDS (though now they are called The Community of Christ), whose first leader was the son of Joseph Smith Jr., Joseph Smith III. This church condemned Polygamy. A small Mormon church named Church of Christ Temple Lot, was able to eventually purchase the plot of land which Joseph Smith Jr. had consecrated to build the main temple, from which the whole Earth would be ruled when Jesus Christ (PBUH) returned, located in Independence, Missouri. James Strang claimed a letter of appointment from Joseph Smith, had his own scripture called the "Book of the Law of the Lord" and led a Mormon church until he was murdered in 1856 C.E. Sidney Rigdon was associated with a Mormon Church in Pennsylvania until his death in 1876 C.E. Modern changes within the Community of Christ have led to a traditional RLDS splinter group and other splinter groups.

At the present time, there are many Mormon Churches, and since the modernization of the Community of Christ, more Restoration groups appear all of the time. The main Utah church (LDS) has over fifteen million members. The Community of Christ as over two hundred thousand. The Church of Christ, Temple Lot has about fifteen thousand. The largest fundamentalist/polygamist Utah splinter group has about five thousand members.

10. The Watchtower Bible & Tract Society was originally founded by Charles Taze Russell (February 16ᵗʰ 1852 C.E. – October 31ˢᵗ 1916 C.E.) in 1881 C.E. under the originally named Zion's Watchtower Tract Society. Two years earlier, Russell had begun publishing the religious journal "Zion's Watch Tower and Herald of Christ's Presence." In doing so, Russell founded the Bible Student Movement. The Bible Students were organized as independent study groups who studied the Bible using the writings of Russell. After Russell's death, the movement split into two groups, the Bible Students Association and what would eventually be called (in 1931 C.E.) the Jehovah's Witnesses, the latter group led authoritatively by Joseph Franklin 'Judge' Rutherford (November 8ᵗʰ 1869 C.E. – January 8ᵗʰ 1942 C.E.). Other Bible Student groups would eventually depart because of changes instituted by Rutherford.

Charles Taze Russell had been raised in Presbyterian and Congregationalist churches. Although a student of the bible in youth, at the age of 16 he began to question his faith. Russell then began to investigate Islam and Eastern Religions although he did not convert to any of them. At the age of 18, Russell heard the teaching of the famous Adventist preacher Jonas Wendell. This encounter renewed Russell's faith in the Bible and gave him a new zeal for preaching the Gospel.

After being rebaptized and studying under Millerite Adventist teachers (who taught the Second Coming of Christ would occur in 1874), Russell obtained a copy of "Herald of the Morning," a publication by Nelson Barbour and in a meeting in Philadelphia. Barbour introduced new ideas to Russell, one of which was that the Second Coming would come to pass in April 1878 C.E. When the Second Coming did not come to pass, Russell and Barbour had an ongoing debate from the Spring of 1878 C.E. through the Summer of 1879 C.E. in the pages of the "herald," then parted ways.

In July 1879 C.E., Russell published the first issue of "Zion's Watch Tower" and "Herald of Christ's Presence." In 1881 C.E., Zion's Watch Tower Tract Society was founded to distribute literature and Bibles. The charter of the society was issued in 1884 C.E. Russell's bible study group had grown very large, while other groups throughout the eastern United States and in other countries began to form. Pastor Russell, as he was now called, was elected pastor every year, a practice followed in other countries also.

Russell published "Food for Thinking Christians" and two other books in 1881 C.E. In 1886 C.E., his most popular book, "(The Divine) Plan of the Ages," was published. This was the first of 6 books in his "Studies in the Scriptures" (originally titled "The Millennial Dawn" series), the last volume of which was published in 1904 C.E.

Russell did not believe in the Trinity, but believed instead that Jehovah was God, Jesus Christ was the incarnation of the Archangel Michael, that Paradise would be on the remade Earth, and that there was no eternal Hell, but that those who rejected the Gospel were annihilated by God. Russell also believed in the coming Millennial Kingdom on Earth. These teachings were the result of Adventist influences. But, unlike the Adventists, Russell believed in what later would be called Zionism, which came from the influence of the Nelson Barbour. Russell taught that Jews should not convert to Christianity, and that Palestine belonged to the Jews. Originally, Russell predicted the Jews would return to Palestine by 1910 C.E. When that didn't happen, Russell used the Jewish press to boldly declare that 1914 C.E. should be the time when Jews boldly reclaim the land of Palestine.

After the death of Charles Taze Russell in 1916 C.E., 'Judge' Rutherford took the reigns of the Watchtower, and as a result of his changes, seventy-five percent of the Bible Students split with the Watchtower, forming various independent Bible Student groups. Under Rutherford, the Watchtower Bible Students changed their name to The Jehovah's Witnesses, and several of Russell's teachings, such as Zionism, were rejected. More about the Jehovah's

Witnesses will be discussed later, in the section on the 20th Century C.E. which follows below. The Bible Students who remained faithfully to Russell's teaching did not grow in size like the Jehovah's Witnesses because they are independent groups with no central leadership. However, many of these groups still exist into the 21st Century C.E.

11. Some developments within the Roman Catholic Church in the 19th Century C.E.

The Oxford Movement within the Anglican Church was a movement by High Churchmen to move the Church of England, many of whom were from the University Oxford, toward its Catholic roots. After the issue of a series of tracts from 1833 C.E. to 1841 C.E., the Oxford Movement also became known as the Tractarian Movement.

Some of the important leaders among the movement's scholars and clergy were Edward Bouverie Pusey, John Kreble, Henry Edward Manning, and John Henry Newman (who argued that the Thirty-Nine Articles of the Church of England were compatible with the Council of Trent). When Newman converted to the Roman Catholic Church in 1845, this brought an end to the Oxford Movement as such, although it would have a considerable influence on the Church of England until the present day. Henry Edward Manning, an Archdeacon, would convert to the Roman Catholic Church.

After converting to the Roman Catholic Church, John Henry Newman (b.1801 C.E. – d. 1891 C.E.) wrote a famous and influential book titled "Apologia Pro Vita Sua," which was a religious autobiography. Newman's Grammar of Assent was probably his most recognized work. Newman was made a Cardinal in the Roman Catholic Church (one who elects a Pope) and is considered one of the most important Roman Catholics of recent centuries.

Two other developments within the Roman Catholic Church deserve mention. In 1854 C.E., Pope Pius IX (b. 1792 C.E. – d. 1879 C.E.), whose reign as Pope was the longest of all the successors of the Apostle Peter (at 31 years), made an infallible decree declaring the Immaculate Conception of the Blessed Virgin Mary (PBUH). Because the Roman Catholic Church's dogma of Original Sin, the view that the Virgin Mary was born without sin had always been taught, but was not previously a dogma that one needed to believe to be a member of the Roman Catholic Church. Some years later, Pope Pius XI called the Vatican I Ecumenical Church Council in 1869-70 C.E. It was not until this Council that the dogma of the Infallibility of the Pope was declared. When the Pope issues a specifically defined official statement Ex Cathedra, or "from the chair of Saint Peter," it becomes a dogma of the Church which must be believed as a matter of Catholic faith. The Vatican I Church Council was not completed because anti-Papal Italian nationalist Victor Emmanuel captured the city of Rome and the Vatican that year (1870 C.E.), signaling the end of the Papal States. Although Emmanuel granted the Law of Guarantees, the Pope was no longer allowed to govern. As a result, Pope Pius IX considered himself a prisoner in the Vatican. The Popes would not be allowed to rule again until 1929 C.E., when Benito Mussolini established Vatican City as a sovereign nation independent of Italy.

EIGHTEEN

Some Developments in American Christianity in the 20th Century.

The 20th Century held many important developments within Christianity. Some of those will be discussed below, including:

- The Fundamentalist Movement
- The Pentecostal Movement and the Charismatic Movement
- The Jehovah's Witnesses
- Armstrong and the Radio Church of God
- Neo-Orthodoxy
- The Vatican II Roman Catholic Ecumenical Church Council

1. The Fundamentalist Movement began at the end of the 19th Century C.E. to combat liberalism and modern philosophy that was gaining headway within Evangelical churches. A forerunner to the Fundamentalist movement may be seen in Downgrade Controversy, which began when the famous Particular Baptist preacher, Charles Haddon Spurgeon (b. June 18th 1834 C.E. – d. January 31st 1892 C.E.) began preaching against the downgrading of the Gospel as preached by liberal pastors. Spurgeon, though self-taught, was not opposed to the study of science and philosophy.

In 1910 C.E., a 12 volume set of books titled "The Fundamentals" and edited by R. A. Torrey was published. Theologians and scholars from various denominations in the USA and the UK contributed articles to the volumes. The articles themselves defended traditional Christian doctrines with carefully thought out arguments, and by criticizing opponents with fairness. Very quickly, however, Fundamentalism took an anti-intellectual turn in many quarters. Many Fundamentalists, especially in the Southern United States, accepted Dispensational Premillennialism. The Fundamentals were reduced to five:

i. The Inerrancy of Scripture

ii. The Virgin Birth of Christ

iii. The Substitution Atonement of Christ

iv. The Bodily Resurrection of Christ

v. The Historicity of Miracles

Some factions substituted The Deity of Jesus Christ for The Virgin Birth and Dispensational Premillenial Doctrine for Historicity of Miracles.

In 1919 C.E., the World's Christian Fundamentals Association was founded. Battles raged between fundamentalists and liberals, dispensationalists and amillenialists, and other various factions in Northern denominations in the USA. Politically, the opposition of Fundamentalists to Darwinian Evolution led to the famous Scopes 'Monkey' trial in 1925 C.E. in Dayton, Tennessee, where William Jennings Bryan, a Presbyterian layman and three-time presidential candidate, led the Fundamentalist cause.

In the 1930s C.E., new denominations and new colleges and ministries were formed by fundamentalists who desired to separate from liberals and modernists in the larger denominations. By the early 1940s C.E., Fundamentalism was essentially split into two camps. On the one hand, some who preferred to call themselves Evangelicals wanted to maintain ties with the larger Protestant denominations. Others who still called themselves Fundamentalists believed they were more faithful to Biblical Christianity than those who called themselves Evangelicals. As a result, Fundamentalists, who themselves fell into different camps, found it hard to co-operate as a whole. Those Christians who belonged to neither groups called both groups Fundamentalists.

In the 1970s-1980s C.E., especially with the election of Ronald Reagan as President of the United States, Fundamentalists became well-known figures nationally. The four most visible of these leaders are Hal Lindsey, Jerry Falwell, Pat Robertson, and Tim LaHaye, all of whom are Christian Zionists.

Hal Lindsey (b. 1929 C.E.), a graduate of Dallas Theological Seminary, had a bestselling book published in 1970 C.E. titled "The Late Great Planet Earth," which eventually sold over fifteen million copies. In this book, Hal Lindsey predicted that the Second Coming of Christ would come to pass in 1988

C.E., based on his interpretation of certain New Testament passages which Hal Lindsey interpreted to mean that Christ would return 40 years after the founding of the modern state of Israel in 1948. Lindsey's timeline was based on the study notes of the "Scofield Reference Bible." Some of Lindsey's other well-known books are "There's a New World Coming," "Satan is Alive and Well and Living on the Planet Earth," and after the World Trade Center bombings in 2001 C.E. "The Everlasting Hatred: The Roots of Jihad" where Lindsey attempts to make the case that the conflict between Islam and the West is grounded in biblical conflict between the children of Jacob (PBUH) and the children of Esau, whom Lindsey identifies with Ishmael (PBUH) the son of Abraham (PBUH). Lindsey interprets Genesis 12:3, "And I will bless them that bless thee, and curse him that curseth thee: and in thee shall all families of the earth be blessed."(KJV), and Genesis 27:29 "Let people serve thee, and nations bow down to thee: be lord over thy brethren, and let thy mother's son's bow down to thee: cursed [be] every one that curseth thee, and blessed [be] he that blesseth thee" (KJV), to mean that Muslims and Arabs (whose forefathers were Ishmael (PBUH) and Esau) are the enemies of the Jews and this will be the doom of Islam.

Jerry Falwell (b. 1933 C.E. – d. 2007 C.E.), a Baptist pastor and televangelist and social activist, founded both the Moral Majority political lobby (in 1979 C.E.) and Liberty University. Although the Moral Majority dissolved in 1989 C.E., its spirit lives on in the Christian Coalition. Jerry Falwell's social activism against pornography and homosexuals led to lawsuits against Penthouse and Hustler magazines for libel, and a lawsuit against Falwell by homosexual activist Jerry Sloan. Known for making controversial remarks, Falwell called the AIDS epidemic "… the wrath of a just God against homosexuals," which angered the homosexual community. After the Twin Tower attacks of 2001 C.E., Falwell made the claim a year later that the Prophet Muhammad (PBUH) was a terrorist and "a violent man, a man of war." Falwell has also claimed on FOX News that the Prophet Muhammad (PBUH) married a 9 year old girl and is therefore a child molester.

Pat Robertson (b. 1930 C.E.), is a Christian televangelist and a Christian right political activist who has founded many organizations. Among these organizations is the Christian Broadcasting Network (CBN), the Christian Coalition, the 700 Club, Regent University. Robertson was an ordained Southern Baptist minister (with a Dispensationalist and Charismatic theology) until 1988 C.E. when he unsuccessfully ran for president of the USA. Like Jerry Falwell, Robertson is known for making controversial statements in the news media. For example, in 2005 C.E., Robertson called for the assassination of Venezuelan President Hugo Chavez, warned the citizens of Dover Pennsylvania of the wrath of God for voting supporters of Intelligent Design off the school board, and accused all critics of the Iraqi War of treason.

Timothy F. LaHaye (b. 1926 C.E.) is a Christian minister and author. He is the co-author (with Jerry B. Jenkins) of the bestselling "Left Behind" series which is Dispensationalist apocalyptic fiction. LaHaye helped found various conservative lobbyist groups. His wife Beverly LaHaye is also a Christian social activist. Even though there are no seminaries anymore who teach the classic version of Dispensationalism, the "Left Behind" series follows the same timeline used by John Darby, C. I. Scofield, and Hal Lindsey, thus keeping classic Dispensationalism the most popular eschatology among Fundamentalist Christians despite the newer versions of Dispensationalism that have appeared in the last few decades.

Not all Dispensational Fundamentalists are controversial. One example is Dr. Jack Van Impe (b. 1930 C.E.), who, with his wife Rexella, hosts the weekly television show Jack Van Impe Presents. Dr. Van Impe is known as 'The Walking Bible' for memorization of the Bible, claiming to have memorized 14,000 verses. Van Impe began his ministry as a Fundamentalist and Dispensationalist Minister, with the same strict approach as any Fundamentalist. Eventually, Dr. Van Impe concluded that the strict Fundamentalist approach was not compatible with the spirit of love he saw in the Bible, and so he moved away from Fundamentalism, receiving criticism for doing so. Van Impe speaks highly of other Evangelicals and other conservative Christian leaders such as Pope John Paul II. After 2001, Van Impe criticized only the terrorists for the 2001 bombings, not all Muslims and Islam, and has dialogued with some Muslim leaders. In 2005 C.E., after Pat Robertson called for the assassination of Hugo Chavez, Van Impe criticized Robertson on Jack Van Impe Presents by stating "we do not need an Osama bin Laden" for a leader.

2. Pentecostalism is a movement that developed as a result of developments within Wesleyan Holiness churches in the last two decades of the 19th Century C.E. Pentecostalism emphasizes the gifts of the Spirit and envisions the 'upper room' experience of the disciples of Jesus Christ (PBUH) as reported in chapter 2 of the Book of the Acts of the Apostles in the New Testament to be an experience as valid today as it was in the 1st Century C.E. Church. The Charismatic Movement that appeared some decades later is very similar to the Pentecostal movement, with the differences that, at least initially, the Charismatic Movement remained in existing Christian denominations, whereas the Pentecostals separated from mainstream Christian denominations. The book "Operation World" which is a guidebook for Christian missionaries estimated that in 2000 C.E., there were 120 million Pentecostals worldwide.

Most Pentecostals view the Baptism of the Holy Spirit as described in the second chapter of the Acts of the Apostles as a 'second work of grace' after a person is born again by believing the Gospel. Other Pentecostals believe that the verse Acts 2:38 gives the plan of salvation as having three steps:

i. Repent (and believe)

ii. Be water-baptized in the name of Jesus

iii. Be filled with the Holy Spirit with the evidence of speaking in tongues

These three steps are believed by many (although not all) of those Pentecostals, who early in the movement rejected the Trinity Doctrine, for the Oneness view of God, similar to the Sabellianism of the 2nd Christian Century C.E., which is the belief that God is one Person, who has three modes or offices (Father, Son and Holy Spirit), and that Jesus Christ (PBUH) is the incarnation of the one God. The largest 'Oneness' denomination is the United Pentecostal Church International (UPCI).

The Pentecostal movement began when Agnes Ozman (1870 C.E. – 1937 C.E.) claimed to have received the gift of tongues at a prayer meeting at Charles Fox Parham's (1873 C.E. – 1929 C.E.) Bethel Bible School in Topeka, Kansas, in 1901 C.E. There were earlier claims of similar phenomena in the years leading up to this, but the Pentecostal movement is usually seen as beginning here. Parham, a Methodist minister, began having revival meetings. William J. Seymour (1970 C.E. – 1922 C.E.), an African American student of Parham, attended these meeting, although as an African-American, Seymour had to remain outside the room where the meeting took place.

In 1906 C.E., the Azusa Street Revival began when William Seymour and others to whom he ministered reported being filled with the Holy Spirit. As the small congregation began to grow, an old African Methodist Episcopal church was rented. Its address at 312 Azusa Street, San Francisco, CA, gave the revival its name. The organization became known as the Apostolic Gospel Mission. The meetings were inter-racial until 1924 C.E., when the Church split upon racial lines. However, integrated meetings continued in other Pentecostal churches, even in the segregated Southern United States.

Many Pentecostal denominations emerged, such as the Assemblies of God, various Churches of God, the Pentecostal Freewill Baptists, the Foursquare Church, and the United Pentecostal Church. In the late 1950s C.E., the Charismatic Movement began to spread in existing denominations. By the mid-1970s C.E., some Charismatic Christians began leaving existing main-line denominations and joining Pentecostal Churches, or forming their own movements (such as the Vineyard Churches and the House-Church Movement in Britain). By the late 1980s C.E., it had become increasingly hard to separate the Charismatic Movement from the Pentecostal Movement. A 'Third Wave of the Holy Spirit' was said to have emerged in the early 1990s C.E. with the Toronto Blessing phenomena and the Word-Faith movement.

Other influences upon Pentecostals were Dispensationalism and the Hebrew Names Movement. Many Pentecostals in the 1920s-30s C.E. used the Scofield Reference Bible as their pulpit Bible. As with several Baptist denominations, one was required to hold a Dispensational view of history and belief in a Pre-Tribulation Rapture of the Church to be ordained as a minister by a these branches of Pentecostalism. To a much lesser degree, the Hebrew Names movement influenced some Pentecostals. Among the influences was the introduction of Hebrew names and terminology and even practices into some Pentecostal Churches. Jesus Christ (PBUH) was referred to as 'Yeshua Hamashiach.' The Festivals of the Torah replaced Christmas and Easter, which were seen as Pagan holidays.

3. The Jehovah's Witnesses is a religious sect of Christianity that traces its roots back to Charles Taze Russell and the Watchtower. As stated in the previous chapter, Judge Rutherford gained control of the Watchtower in 1917 after the death of Russell. About three-fourths of the Bible Student groups broke with the Watchtower because of changes instituted by Rutherford, who desired to bring in all existing Bible Student groups under the government of the Watchtower. The Zionism of Russell was discarded. New books on official teachings replaced the 6 Volume Studies in the Scriptures series penned by Russell. The Singing of Hymns was even abandoned for several years. In 1931, the Bible Students still with the Watchtower, adopted the name Jehovah's Witnesses taken from a part of the Bible verse Isaiah 43:10, "You are my witnesses, is the utterance of Jehovah..." as it reads in the New World Translation of the Bible. The New World Translation of the New Testament first appeared in 1950 C.E. The translation of the entire Bible was published in 1961 C.E.

Jehovah's Witnesses worship at a building they call the Kingdom Hall rather than call the building a Church. Adult Believer's Baptism is practiced.

The magazines "The Watchtower" and "Awake" are distributed by Jehovah's Witnesses, each of which is called a Publisher because of the books they sell. All time spent in evangelism is reported. Jehovah's Witnesses may move upward in the hierarchy of the Church Government for being active in evangelism. The book sold in the late 1990 C.E. to present basic Watchtower teachings is called Knowledge. Jehovah's Witnesses traditionally shared the gospel by going door to door in pairs but other methods are practiced nowadays. Witnesses will offer bible studies in homes, and book studies in members' homes. At the Kingdom hall, there is the main weekly service as well as other classes. Conferences are held annually in Spring and Fall. The only celebration is Passover, at which only those who believe that they will be among the 144,000 who actually go to Heaven partake of the Lord's Supper.

Jehovah's Witnesses still believe Jehovah is the only True and Eternal God. Like the Arian Christians, Jesus Christ (PBUH) is a created being, the Word of God, the Incarnation of the Archangel Michael. The Holy Spirit is considered God's active force, and is not considered to be a divine Person. Unlike Arians, Jehovah's Witnesses do not worship Jesus Christ. Other beliefs are the Unconscious State of the Dead, Paradise on Earth in the Millennium following the Second Coming of Christ, and Annihilation of the Wicked in the Lake of Fire, for there is no belief in Eternal Torment. Witnesses are not allowed to serve in the military, nor receive blood transfusions. There were an estimated 6.6 million practicing Jehovah's Witnesses in 2005 C.E.

4. Herbert W. Armstrong (1892 C.E. – 1996 C.E.) founded the Radio Church of God, which latter became know as the Worldwide Church of God. Armstrong also established Ambassador College, published the "Plain Truth" magazine, began the World Tomorrow radio show, and authored several books and booklets.

While working in the advertising field in the state of Oregon, Armstrong's wife Loma came to believe in the Seventh Day Sabbath after befriending a woman who was a member of the Church of God, Seventh Day. Armstrong, at that time an agnostic and unfamiliar with the Bible, believed he could demonstrate that the Bible somewhere taught that Sunday should be kept as the Sabbath. When he could not do so, Armstrong became a believer and hence he was baptized in 1927 C.E. Armstrong and his wife then joined the Church of God Seventh Day. In 1930 C.E., their youngest child, Garner Ted Armstrong (d. 2003 C.E.), who would become a well known television personality, was born. The next year, Herbert W. Armstrong was ordained as a minister in the Oregon Conference of the Church of God, which split in 1933 C.E. Armstrong went with the faction led by J. N. Dugger (1886 C.E. – 1975 C.E.).

Armstrong soon began teaching that the Torah Festivals taught in the Book of Leviticus, Chapter 23, ought to be celebrated by all true Christians. His superiors said they agreed with the doctrine, but that not all members did, so Armstrong could not teach the necessity of keeping these holy days. Armstrong then decided to break with the Church of God and work on his own. Armstrong began broadcasting as the Radio Church of God in 1933 C.E. The Church of God, Seventh Day revoked Armstrong's ministerial license in 1937 C.E. In 1946 C.E., Armstrong moved his headquarters to Pasadena, California, where the Radio Church of God was incorporated. The name was changed to The Worldwide Church of God in 1968 C.E.

Some of the basic beliefs taught by Armstrong include:

i.   That God is composed of two co-eternal divine Persons, the Father and the Son.

ii. The Holy Spirit is the power of God.

iii. One who believes the Gospel and becomes a member of the Worldwide Church of God and is faithful with the practices is 'begotten from above,' that is, a seed is planted in the believer. When the believer is raised from the dead and glorified, that is when the believer is born again.

iv. The Ten Commandments, the Dietary Laws, the Leviticus 23 Festivals, and tithing (without Year of Jubilee), but not circumcision, are all required to be practiced by the true believer. Christmas and Easter are considered Pagan holidays adopted by the early Catholic Church.

v.   After the Crucifixion, Jesus Christ was in the ground exactly three days and three nights, and rose again just before sunset on Sabbath evening. Therefore, the crucifixion happened in the afternoon of the Fourth Day of the week (i.e. Wednesday afternoon). Thus, Good Friday and Holy Saturday are not supported by the Bible, nor is Easter.

vi. The Roman Catholic and therefore Protestant Churches are false churches.

vii. Jesus Christ will come and the Millennium will begin at this time. Christ will rule the whole earth from Jerusalem. Greater Israel's boundaries will be the Nile and Euphrates rivers. Christ will demand that representatives from all nations come to Jerusalem to celebrate the Feast of Tabernacles.

viii. The Resurrection and Judgment will happen during the entire Millennium. All those who did not understand the Gospel properly will be given a chance to understand and believe and repent and submit unto the Gospel during this time.

ix. After the Millennium, there will be a New Heaven and a New Earth. Those believers who persevered to the end will rule and reign with Jesus Christ over the whole universe in resurrected perfect bodies.

x. Herbert W. Armstrong was God's representative on Earth.

xi. Joseph's sons Ephraim and Manasseh in prophecy are England and the United States (i.e. Anglo-Israelism).

Herbert W. Armstrong wrote books and booklets. Some of the most well known (and some of which may have been ghost-written by his son Garner Ted Armstrong) are:

i. The Mystery of the Ages

ii. The Wonderful World Tomorrow

iii. The Missing Dimension in Sex

iv. A two volume Autobiography.

v. The Incredible Human Potential

vi. The United States and Britain in Prophecy.

Garner Ted Armstrong, the youngest child of Herbert and Loma Armstrong, became the face of the Worldwide Church of God in the 1960s C.E., when he began appearing on the television show "The World Tomorrow." A good speaker with a charismatic personality, Garner Ted became second in the organization after his father Herbert. Garner Ted became entangled in several scandals and was eventually disfellowshipped for good in 1978 C.E., when he began The Church of God, International. There would be another scandal in which Garner Ted would be forced out of the Church of God, International and form yet another organization, the Intercontinental Church of God in 1995 C.E. Garner Ted Armstrong passed away in 2003 C.E.

Meanwhile, the Worldwide Church of God without Garner Ted became entangled with problems of its own. From 1979-1981 C.E., the Attorney General of California investigated the WCG because of complaints by disgruntled members. Then, in 1986 C.E., Joseph W. Tkach Sr. was appointed

Armstrong's successor and Pastor General of the WCG. From 1986 to 1995 C.E., Joseph W. Tkach instituted several doctrinal changes, which were not accepted by all ministers. In 1989 C.E., Gerald Flurry and John Ames were disfellowshipped and went on to form the Philadelphia Church of God. In 1992 C.E., Evangelist Roderick C. Meredith left to become the Pastor General of the Global Church of God. When larger doctrinal changes came in 1993 C.E., such as the teaching of the Trinity instead of the Binity doctrine, more ministers and lay members became skeptical of the church leadership until finally in 1995 C.E., many members left to form the United Church of God. This same year, Joseph W. Tkach Sr. passed away and was succeeded by his son Joseph Tkach Jr., who was appointed Pastor General. At this point, the Worldwide Church of God has virtually the same doctrines as many Trinitarian Evangelical churches. Several hundred splinter groups were formed by former members of the WCG, ranging in size from several thousand members to just a few families who meet in homes.

In 1997 C.E., after the Philadelphia Church of God reprinted Herbert W. Armstrong's book "The Mystery of the Ages" which had been out of print for several years, the Worldwide Church of God sued the Philadelphia Church of God for copyright infringement. The PCG claimed that the volume is a necessary religious book for the Church. Although in 2000 C.E. the Ninth Circuit Court of Appeals ruled that the PCG infringed upon the copyright and awarded damages to the WCG, the suit finally settled in 2003 C.E. when WCG sells the rights for "Mystery of the Ages" and nineteen other copyrighted sold books to the PCA for 3 million dollars.

In the final analysis, Herbert W. Armstrong and the teachings of the Worldwide Church of God had a pronounced impact in some quarters of Evangelical Christianity in the late 20th Century C.E. In 1969, when Australian Michael Dennis Rohan attempted to set fire to the Al-Aqsa mosque on the Temple Mount in Jerusalem, he claimed his actions were influenced by the teachings of Herbert W. Armstrong's book, 1975 In Prophecy!, which was written and published in 1956 C.E., and by various editorials in the freely distributed Plain Truth Publication. In a 1967 C.E. Plain Truth article, Armstrong did write that he believed the Temple in Jerusalem would be rebuilt and animal sacrifices would be once again performed in "about four-and-a-half years." Armstrong's response was to state that the claim by Rohan was meant to do damage to the work of Armstrong and the Worldwide Church of God, and that Rohan was not even a member of the WCG. Armstrong went on to reject the teaching that the Temple would be rebuilt in that time.

Several Evangelical and Pentecostal groups, as the result of Armstrong's teaching on the 7th Day Sabbath and the Leviticus 23 festivals, as well as the Millennial rule of Jesus Christ (PBUH) from Jerusalem, have incorporated the celebration of the 7th Day Sabbath and Jewish Festivals, and in some cases even the dietary laws, into their practices.

5. The theological school of Neo-Orthodoxy appeared soon after World War I (1914 C.E. – 1918 C.E.). The movement was a response to the Protestant Liberalism that appeared in Europe in the 1800s C.E. The major proponent of the movement was Swiss Reformed Theologian Karl Barth (1886 C.E. – 1968 C.E.), who was the most important Reformed thinker since John Calvin. Other well-known theologians associated with the movement were Emil Brunner (1899 C.E. – 1966 C.E.), and Robert Bultmann (1884 C.E. – 1976 C.E.). Though not a completely unified movement, due to major differences of opinion between leaders within the movement, there were four points in which advocates found degrees of agreement. They are:

    i.   Strong Emphasis on the Revelation of God against Natural Theology.

    ii. The Transcendence of God.

    iii. Existentialism (especially from a Christian perspective).

    iv. The Sinful Nature of Humanity, especially as could be seen in the First World War.

It should be noted that neo-Orthodoxy is a movement within Christianity distinct from both Protestant Liberalism and Fundamentalism. Karl Barth, for instance rejected both the doctrine of Scriptural Inerrancy of the Fundamentalists on the one hand, and the view of modernist Christians of the same time who believed God could be known through human scholarship. Barth believed the Bible was the main source of God's Word understandable by humanity. One needed to read the Bible and existentially make a leap of faith to understand God's Word.

Born in Basel, Germany, Barth spent his early life in Germany. He pastored a church from 1911 C.E. to 1921 C.E. and later was professor of theology in Bonn. In 1935 C.E., after refusing to swear allegiance to Hitler, Barth had to leave Germany, and so he moved back to Basel where he became a professor. Barth's most well known works are his "Commentary on the Epistle of Romans," of which the second edition appeared in 1922 C.E., and his 13-volume "Church Dogmatics," which was started in 1932 C.E. and had six million words when he died in 1968. It is the largest such work ever written.

Some scholars have joked that, for a theologian who stressed the immanence of God, Barth sure had a lot to say about God. Lastly, Karl Barth was largely responsible for writing the "Barmen Declaration," in which Lutheran and Reformed Churches addressed problems that stemmed from the Third Reich. The influence of the Nazis was to be rejected by the Church, whose allegiance is to the God of Jesus Christ, not to other 'lords.'

In the United States, Barth was not so well accepted by conservative Evangelicals and Fundamentalists, because while Barth did believe the essential dogmas of Christianity, Barth rejected what they considered the most important dogma of all, the inerrancy of Scripture. In later life, Barth lectured at Princeton University. He was invited to attend the Vatican II Church Council, but had to decline due to illness.

6. The Vatican II Ecumenical Church Council was called by Pope John XXIII in 1962 C.E., and was concluded in 1965 C.E. by Pope Paul VI. Pope John XXIII was once quoted as saying he wanted to open the window and let some "fresh air" into the Church. After Vatican I, and in reaction to the Modernist heresy within the Church, there had been an emphasis on Neo-Scholasticism and Biblical Literalism. New theologians such as Karl Rahner and including Joseph Ratzinger (now Pope Benedict XVI), wanted a renewed Christian dogma which made room for modern human experience. The Church could be refreshed through a more accurate understanding of scripture and the early Church Fathers. There is not space to write an in-depth description of the Vatican II Council. However, some results will be mentioned following.

i.   The Liturgy of the Western (Latin) Rite (known as the Tridentine Mass because of the standardization of the Mass that was implemented as a result of the Council of Trent) was rewritten and celebrated in the vernacular language instead of Latin. There was more participation by the lay people in the Mass. Even the layout of the altar changed in many churches. The priest began to celebrate the Mass facing the congregation. The tabernacle where the sacrament was kept (i.e. bread and wine that had been consecrated and was now the Body and Blood of Christ) was now sometimes placed at the side of the altar, instead of on the altar in the center. Also, the Divine Office (prayers at various hours of the day) was revamped and prayed in the vernacular language instead of Latin.

ii. The Dogmatic Constitution of the Church (Lumen Gentium – Light of the Nations) is perhaps the most well-known document to come from Vatican II. Chapter one deals with the traditional Four Marks of the True Church (i.e. One, Holy, Catholic, and Apostolic) which is ruled by the successor of Peter, the Pope, and the bishops who are in communion with the Pope. This chapter also makes the admission that sanctification and truth can be found outside the Church. Chapter two teaches that the Will of God is to save people both as individuals and as people groups (such as ancient Israel). While all human beings are called to join the True Church, not all are fully within the bounds of the Church, and do not profess with completeness the Catholic faith, these humans are still joined in many ways to the Church (Eastern Orthodox and Protestants), and there are even some points of joining with others, such as Muslims and Jews, who are explicitly mentioned in the text. Chapter three, titled "the Church is Hierarchal," defines the role of bishops and the Pope. The other chapters discuss the Laity, the call to holiness in the Church, religious orders, the Pilgrim Church (i.e. the Church on the Earth in the present time), and the Blessed Virgin Mary. Lumen Gentium was one of many documents to come from Vatican II. As might be expected, The Vatican II council has been criticized by most Traditionalist Catholics. Some traditionalists have gone so far as to say that the leaders of the Roman Catholic Church have fallen into heresy, and some even go so far as to say the Chair of Peter (the Office of the Pope who is the Successor of Peter) is vacant. The Ultra-Traditionalists are called "Sedevacantists" from two Latin words meaning (The Chair (of Peter) is vacant). Very small groups of Ultra-Traditionalists have even elected their own 'Pope.' Of the many documents produced as a result of Vatican II, four, including Lumen Gentium, are Dogmatic Constitutions. Three are Dogmatic Declarations, and nine are Dogmatic Decrees.

iii. Humanae Vitae (Latin for One Human Life) was a post-conciliar (post Vatican II) document promulgated by Pope Paul VI in 1968 C.E. "The Encyclical," the title of which is usually translated into English as "On the Regulation of Human Birth" gives the official Roman Catholic position on abortion, contraception, and other topics regarding human life. Humanae Vitae forbids abortion, sterilization, and every action intended to prevent procreation, but allows natural family planning methods, such as abstaining from sexual intercourse during certain times in the woman's cycle. The encyclical points out that the Church cannot make lawful what is unlawful. It is controversial, even within the Roman Catholic Church, because it prohibits the use of birth control.

iv. The Tridentine Mass of the Roman Missal promulgated by Pope Pius V in 1570 C.E. and its successive forms in use until 1962 C.E. (although some do not include the Missal of Pope John XXIII of 1962 C.E.) was replaced by the Mass of Pope Paul VI in 1970 C.E. Many Traditionalist Catholics did not agree with this development of Vatican II. Some groups, such as the Society of (Pope) Saint Pius X (SSPX), founded in 1970 C.E. under the leadership of Archbishop Lefebvre, continued to celebrate the Tridentine Mass. When Archbishop Lefebvre ordained bishops without permission in 1988 C.E., he (and therefore the Society) were excommunicated from the Roman Catholic Church. While the SSPX priests still pray for the Pope during the Mass, a breakaway group called the SSPV (Society of (Pope) Saint Pius V) does not pray for the Pope during Mass and are known as Sedevacantists. In 1984 C.E., Pope John Paul II allowed the celebration of the Pre-1970 C.E. Roman Missal. In his 1988 C.E. letter Ecclesia Dei, Pope John Paul II allowed for the celebration of the pre-1970 C.E. Roman Missal, stating that "respect must everywhere be shown for the feelings of all those who are attached to the Latin liturgical tradition." The authorization of the 1962 C.E. Roman Missal can be granted either by the Holy See or by the Bishop of the Diocese where the Mass is requested to be celebrated. Some bishops do not grant permission, however. The Fraternal Society of St. Peter (FSSP) is a priestly society in full communion with the Roman Catholic Church which came into being as a result of the letter Ecclesia Dei. Very recently, Pope Benedict XVI has given permission for any priest to celebrate the 1962 Missal.

v. As a result of Vatican II, the Charismatic Movement, the spread of Dispensational Fundamentalism as a result of bestselling books by Hal Lindsey and others, and even the 'Hippie' counter-culture movement, many Roman Catholics left the Church beginning in the late 1960s C.E. Beginning in 1990 C.E., some Evangelical and Charismatic Christians began converting and even returning to the Roman Catholic Church. Some well-known Evangelicals who became Roman Catholic are Dr. Scott and Kimberly Hahn (both born 1957 C.E.) and Gerry Mattatics.

vi. The Eastern Orthodox Church saw a similar though smaller movement somewhat earlier. The Evangelical Orthodox Church (EOC), which was the eventual result of a 'House-Church' movement founded by Campus Crusade for Christ evangelical missionary Peter E. Gillchrist (b.1938 C.E.) in 1973 C.E. to restore primitive Christianity, joined the Antiochian Christian Orthodox Archdiocese of North America in 1987 C.E. Some of its churches waited until later to join the Orthodox Church in America. A few have remained independent and still use the EOC name.

Conclusions:

I. Christianity (after Jesus Christ (PBUH) was off the scene) was never a monolithic religion. One movement of Christianity emerged who claimed to have the orthodox faith and practice (i.e. the Catholic Church in the 4th Century). That movement did so with the backing of a powerful government, the Roman Empire. Almost every other movement was either extinguished or eventually died out.

II. The original Christians were Palestinian Jews. The Gospel presented by Jesus Christ (PBUH) exhorted the Jews to repent and turn back to Jehovah, the One Eternal True God, and to practice the Torah of Moses from right intentions, in love (with charity). Human Sacrifice as a sin offering was never taught by any prophets according to the Hebrew Scriptures. Even when Jehovah commanded Abraham (PBUH) to sacrifice his son, Jehovah did not allow Abraham to sacrifice his son, but instead supplied an animal to be slaughtered. Now, if Jehovah shows this kind of mercy to the son of another, doesn't it follow that Jehovah would show more mercy to His own son (if Jehovah had one)?

III. Saul of Tarsus, later known as Paul, borrowed some elements from Mystery Religions that existed in the Roman Empire in the First Century C.E. and adopted them to the Gospel originally taught by Jesus Christ (PBUH). Paul proclaimed himself to be an apostle, thereby claiming that he had the same authority as the Twelve Apostles chosen by Jesus Christ (PBUH). The Gospel, as propagated by Paul, is described the preaching of 'Christ and him crucified' as opposed to the Gospel of Repentance toward God (or Kingdom of God in the believer's heart) preached by John the Baptist (PBUH) and Jesus Christ (PBUH). Like the previous suffering God-men in previous Mystery Religions (such as the Osiris, Dionysus, Orpheus Bacchus, Attus, and Tammuz), the death of Christ benefits believers in the 'mystery' of Godliness.

IV. Christians who read the writings of Paul, and the "Gospel and Epistles" attributed to John, after the fact, attempted to explain the relationship of the Father, Son, and Holy Spirit in different ways. The view eventually defined by Athanasius at the 1st Ecumenical Council (Nicaea I) in 325 C.E., appears to be a hybrid of the view advanced by early Trinitarians such as Tertullian, and the Modalistic Monarchians such as Noetus and Sabellius. Tertullian believed that the Father and Son (and Holy Spirit) were a unity of distinct co-eternal persons of like substance. Sabellius believed that the Father, Son, and Holy Spirit were of the same substance, but were one Divine Person incarnated as Jesus Christ. Athanasius followed Tertullian in teaching that the Father and the Son were distinct co-eternal Divine Persons, yet followed Sabellius in teaching that the Father and the Son were of the same substance. When Constantine, who had called Nicaea I, saw that the Athanasian party were actually a minority, and that (as Jerome reported), eighty percent of the Empire held the view of Pope (which the Athanasians had labeled the Semi-Arian heresy – since Arius taught that the Son was created and therefore of a different substance than the Father), Constantine joined the Semi-Arian party. Constantine was baptized on his death bed by Bishop Eusebius, a Semi-Arian who wrote the important "Ecclesiastical History." After a succession of Semi-Arian emperors followed by Julian the 'Apostate' who wanted to revive a charitable paganism, Theodosius the Great, an Athanasian, became Emperor and declared that one must hold the Catholic faith to be a citizen of the Roman Empire. This was a death-blow not only to the Semi-Arians, but also to all Christian sects within the Roman Empire who did not hold the Athanasian view of the Trinity.

V. The twenty-seven books of the 'Canonical' New Testament were not ever listed in exactly that form until circa 363 C.E. when Athanasius, then Bishop of Alexandria, gave this list in a pastoral letter to the churches in his diocese. Athanasius also suggested that the "Didache" and "the Shepherd of Hermas," two books that were considered scripture in more Christian centers than some of the books finally selected for the New Testament, were good for private reading. At the Council of Carthage in North Africa in 397 C.E., the same 27 books suggested by Athanasius were selected as the final 'canon' or authorized list for the Catholic Church in the West. This same 'canon' was ratified at the Ecumenical Council of Ephesus in 430 C.E. by the Catholic Church throughout the Roman Empire.

VI. Original Sin

The Augustinian doctrine of Original Sin as taught in Western Christianity did not exist as such until the beginning of the 5th Century C.E., as a result of the Pelagian Controversy. Pelagius, a British monk who was raised in a Christian home, was concerned about the state of the souls of his ancestors who lived before Christianity reached Britain. Pelagius and his followers taught that man is born well, fully able to please God by following Christ's example. Augustine of Hippo, who had been a Manichaean until reading

Plotinus, the well-known neo-Platonic philosopher who had lived in the previous century. After reading Plotinus, Augustine was again able to read the "Epistles of Paul" and became a Christian through the preaching of Ambrose of Milan. Augustine made use of neo-Platonic thought in his criticism of Pelagianism. Augustine taught that Adam's sin was passed to his progeny because Adam (PBUH) was the Natural Head of the human race. Therefore, all men sinned and fell from grace when Adam (PBUH) sinned. Only if God chooses to extend His grace to a person can that person be saved. A human being on his own can still make choices, but cannot choose to please God.

It should be said that this new teaching was not present in the earliest writings of Augustine, or any Church father before him. John Cassian, a French monk who entered the discussion between Augustinians and Pelagians, took a middle view. John Cassian criticized Pelagius for teaching that man was born well and could obey God without the need for God's grace. Cassian also criticized Augustine for introducing the notion that all men were guilty of Original Sin. Cassian's views of man and sin were similar to those of the earlier Church Fathers. Cassian believed that man was born weak, sick with sin, but still could co-operate with God's grace given to all. A man was guilty of sin when he actually sinned.

The Western Church at the Council of Orange in the 6th century condemned Pelagianism, condemned writings of John Cassian that pertained to the controversy, but not Cassian himself, who was canonized as a saint (as was Augustine). The council affirmed most but not all of Augustine's teachings. John Cassian's views were accepted by the Eastern Catholics.

VII. The Theory of the Atonement.
The popular theory of the atonement in conservative Western Christianity at the beginning of the 21st Century was not taught by anyone in Christianity until Anselm of Canterbury's work "Cur Deus Homo" ("Why the God-man?") appeared in 1098 C.E. It was similar to, but not identical to, the view of the Atonement taught by the Protestant Reformers. This view, which states that God the Father's holiness and honor were offended by Adam's Original Sin, and therefore needed to be paid off by the atonement of Christ, was never known by the Eastern Church.

VIII. Dispensationalism as taught by Darby, Scofield, Lindsey, and Ryrie.
Dispensational Pre-millennial Pre-tribulation Rapture eschatology did not exist until the 1820s C.E. Yet, this very late-appearing theory is the most popular eschatological view in Western Christianity. Some Fundamentalist Dispensationalists will say that this view is present in the writings of the

early Church Father Justin Martyr. It is true that Justin Martyr, like many (but certainly not all) pre-Nicene Church Fathers, believed that the Second Coming of Jesus Christ (PBUH) ushers in the Millennium. However, Justin Martyr firmly declares that the Church is Israel. Dispensationalism teaches that national Israel and the Church of Christ are not the same thing. In fact, some Dispensationalists have gone so far as to accuse Christians in past centuries of being anti-Semitic for holding a Covenantal view of the Church (i.e. that the Church is not Israel).

IX. Proposition.
There has been considerable development of dogma since the 1ˢᵗ Century C.E.

For instance, if you believe these propositions:

1. God is a Trinity of distinct Divine Persons which are of the 'same' substance.

2. The exact 27-book canon of the New Testament.

3. Original Sin.

4. The Atonement of Christ was necessary to pay off the offended God the Father's anger over mankind's sin.

5. The Dispensational Pre-Millennial Pre-Tribulation Rapture view of the Second Coming.

Then you believe it was necessary that:

1. Almost two centuries passed before anyone used the word Trinity to describe the Godhead, and one more century passed before someone who would come up with the definitive formula for the Trinity, and a half a century would pass before that definition became the official teaching of the state Church of Imperial Rome.

2. Although at least 10 of the Letters of Paul were considered canonical by about 100 C.E., and the 4 Gospels were selected by 200 C.E., the entire 27 book New Testament Canon was not suggested as it is until the mid-4ᵗʰ Century C.E., and not accepted by all of the Western Church until just before 400 C.E.

3. It would take until 400 C.E. for the doctrine of Original Sin to be first taught, and then only accepted in the Western Church.

4. It would take over a millennium (almost 1100 C.E.) for anyone to suggest that the atonement of Christ was necessary to buy off the anger of the offended God the Father.

5. It would take 1800 years (almost 2 millennia!) for anyone to develop the Dispensationalism system of theology and eschatology!

Therefore, if Jesus Christ (PBUH) were to return today, would he recognize this Church?

Jesus Christ (PBUH) in Islam is not affected by all of this doctrinal development. In fact, the Muslim Jesus is very much the same Jesus as is described by Palestinian Jewish Christian sects who either did not accept Paul of Tarsus as an apostle (Ebionites, Elchaisites, Nazareans), or those who tolerated Paul of Tarsus but did not take doctrine from him (Jewish Nazoreans). Even in the New Testament documents accepted by Roman Catholic, Orthodox, Protestant, and 'Reconstructionist' Christians (i.e. those who seek to reconstruct the First Century C.E. Church as they believed it existed) show that there were major controversies between the Jerusalem Church and Paul.

Thus, we conclude that the true historical Jesus is the same Jesus Christ (PBUH) that is described in the Quran.

APPENDIX I.
Paul and the
Doctrine of the Trinity.

(Note: Also see discussion on the Gospel of the Hebrews
at the beginning of Chapter XI).

Although neither the word Trinity, nor the phrase 'one God in three Persons' appears anywhere in the Bible, the vast majority of Christians believe this doctrine is to be found in the Bible. Since pre-Christian Israel never believed in a Trinity, the doctrine must have appeared after the Gospel began to be preached.

The majority of the scriptures used to defend the Trinity by seminary-educated Christian scholars appear in the New Testament letters of Paul, and the Gospel and Letters attributed to the Apostle John (which was most likely written after Paul was off the scene). Since the Eastern Christians believe John was quite old at the time the Gospel bearing his name was written, and that John dictated to a younger person who was fluent in Greek, it may be that the "Gospel of John" is a composite document which contain his remembrances, as well as material from other sources and a hymn which comprises the first half of the first chapter of John's Gospel. In fact, this is the view of many modern biblical scholars. (See Dr. Bart Ehrman's book "The New Testament: A Historical Introduction to the Early Christian Writings")

Returning to the New Testament writings of Paul of Tarsus, some history should be given of Paul's conversion to Christianity. Initially, Paul is introduced as a Pharisee named Saul who is persecuting Christian converts from Judaism by order of the High Priest, a Sadducee. This is an interesting point, since Paul claims to be a Pharisee who sat at the feet of the famous Rabbi Gamaliel. However, earlier in the Book of Acts, when Peter and John were in prison for preaching the Gospel, Gamaliel and the Pharisaic party in the Sanhedrin (the Palestinian Jewish ruling body in Jerusalem) were able to thwart a Sadducee attempt to have the apostles put to death. Thus, Paul seems to have more in common with the Sadducees than with Gamaliel and the Pharisees. (See Hyam Jaccoby's book "The Mythmaker: Paul and the Invention of Christianity.")

It is well known from Christian writings that the earliest Christians were Jewish Christians. The Ebionites, for instance, were a Jewish Messianic sect who believed that Jesus Christ (PBUH) was a prophet who was born of two righteous Jews. The Ebionites believed Jesus Christ (PBUH) was killed for preaching the Gospel, but they did not believe his death was a literal atonement for sin, since the Hebrew Scriptures nowhere speak of making human sacrifices to God for the forgiveness of sins. Also, the Ebionites rejected Paul of Tarsus as a false apostle. They believed that Paul had an interest in the daughter of the High Priest of the Temple in Jerusalem, and as a result persecuted the Christians. When the daughter of the High Priest rejected Paul, this is when Paul 'converted' to the cause of the Gospel. Paul declared himself an Apostle to the Gentiles, teaching things the Ebionites and other Palestinian Jewish sects could never accept (as seen in Against Heresies 1.26.2 by Irenaeus; Panarion 16.9 by Epiphanius of Salamis).

A good case can be made that Paul presented the Gospel to Gentiles in such a way that the non-Jews within the Roman Empire would be converted. Gentiles would not be interested in a Jewish Messiah and the law given by Moses (PBUH), but might be interested in a 'Christ' that in some ways resembled other historical and mythological figures known from various mystery religions whose adherents lived within the Roman Empire.

In making this case, the path taken by Sir James George Frazier in his 1922 book "The Golden Bough," which has been since found to be based on many questionable documents, is to be mostly avoided. Instead, the attempt will be made to show that Paul of Tarsus adds some elements from ancient Mystery Religions to the Gospel, which transforms the "Gospel of Repentance" into Paul's "Gospel of Christ Crucified."

'Son of God' in Semitic Languages (Hebrew, Aramaic, Arabic)

In Semitic languages, the terms 'father' and 'son' can be used when a certain person with the means to do so takes care of a group of people. In this usage, the "'father of the house' takes care of a group of people, each of whom are dependants of the 'father,' despite the fact that most or all of these people are not the biological children of the 'father of the house.'" In the Hebrew Scriptures, one such use of the relationship between God and the House of Israel can be found in the "Book of Exodus." This passage is from the English Standard Version:

"Exodus 4:22 Then you shall say to Pharaoh, 'Thus says the LORD, Israel is my firstborn son'"

"Exodus 4:23 and I say to you, 'Let my son go that he may serve me.' If you refuse to let him go, behold, I will kill your firstborn son."

The LORD (which, when all capitals are used, is the translation of Jehovah in many English translations) considers the nation of Israel at the time of Moses (PBUH) as to be His 'firstborn son.' This is because the LORD took care of the nation (or house) of Israel at the time of Moses (PBUH). This passage obviously does not mean that the LORD physically gave birth to the men and women of the nation of Israel.

Numbers 23:19 states: God is not a man, that he should lie, or a son of man, that he should change his mind. Has he said, and will he not do it? Or has he spoken, and will he not fulfill it?

Since like gives birth to like, even if God would physically father some children, which was not a belief of Israel at the time of Moses (PBUH), any children would be Gods. However, these passages demonstrate that God does not have literal children.

Isaiah 43:11 I, "I am the LORD, and besides me there is no savior."

Isaiah 45:21 "Declare and present your case; let them take counsel together! Who told this long ago? Who declared it of old? Was it not I, the LORD?

And there is no other god besides me, a righteous God and a Savior; there is none besides me."

Now, if the LORD God calls Israel His firstborn son, and there is no God or Savior besides the LORD God, and that God is neither a man nor a son of man, then what do we make of passages in the New Testament that claim Jesus Christ (PBUH) is the son of God? The answer is an easy one: the LORD God has the same relationship with Jesus Christ (PBUH) that He had with Israel in the time of Moses (PBUH). The LORD God by a miracle caused the Blessed Virgin Mary (PBUH) to become pregnant, so that a virgin bore a son who was given God's Word and God's Holy Spirit. Jesus Christ (PBUH) was, and is a prophet of God (and therefore a member of God's 'house'), and has given this prophet all the knowledge and wisdom necessary to preach and live the Gospel.

As far as the claims made by those who believe the son of God is also God the Son, either the co-eternal second Divine Person in a Trinity, or a one of three Divine Modes within one Divine Person, one should look at what the word Christ actually means. "Christ from the Greek" word Christos which means 'anointed one,' and is the literal translation of Hebrew word Meshiach or as we say in English, Messiah. By using this title 'anointed one,' the clear meaning is that Jesus (PBUH) is 'the anointed one,' rather than the 'One who does the anointing.' If Jesus is 'the Anointer,' then his title would not be 'Christ,' because then Jesus would be the one doing the anointing, and that is clearly not the title used in the New Testament.

Thus, when Jesus Christ (PBUH) states:

Matthew 20:23 He said to them, "You will drink my cup, but to sit at my right hand and at my left is not mine to grant, but it is for those for whom it has been prepared by my Father."

Jesus is stating that, contrary to the Western view of the Trinity doctrine that the Son is co-equal with the Father, this is indeed not so. In fact, we would expect the One True God, by definition, to be able to do anything within His perfect moral character. Since Jesus (PBUH) states he cannot do something that the Father can do, not only is 'the son' not coequal with the Father, but 'the son' cannot be eternal God, otherwise he would have the right to fulfill this request.

Jesus also declares the following:

Matthew 19:17 and he said to him, "Why do you ask me about what is good? There is only one who is good. If you would enter life, keep the commandments."

John's Gospel, which is written after Paul composed his letters, and has the famous "I AM" passages that most Christians use to claim that the son is co-equal and co-eternal with the Father, has this interesting passage:

John 5:30-31 "I can do nothing on my own. As I hear, I judge, and my judgment is just, because I seek not my own will but the will of him who sent me. If I alone bear witness about myself, my testimony is not deemed true."

These verses can be used to make the case that Jesus Christ (PBUH) is not 'God the Son,' co-eternal and co-equal with the Father, but rather a creature who is dependant upon God for everything and one who wisely chooses to submit unto God.

Turning to a sampling of passages found in the letters written by Paul of Tarsus to various mid-first-century churches, we see that Jesus Christ (PBUH) is described in ways that are different from other parts of the Bible. The Gospel Paul preached that not only "From that time Jesus began to preach, saying, 'Repent, for the kingdom of heaven is at hand'" as is written in Matthew 4:17, but also:

I Corinthian 2:1-2 "And I, when I came to you, brothers[4], did not come proclaiming to you the testimony[5] of God with lofty speech or wisdom. For, I decided to know nothing among you except Jesus Christ and him crucified."

Romans 3: 21-27 "But now the righteousness of God has been manifested apart from the law, although the Law and the Prophets bear witness to it— the righteousness of God through faith in Jesus Christ for all who believe. For there is no distinction: for all have sinned and fall short of the glory of God, and are justified by his grace as a gift, through the redemption that is in Christ Jesus, whom God put forward as a propitiation by his blood, to be received by faith. This was to show God's righteousness, because in his divine forbearance he had passed over former sins. It was to show his righteousness at the present time, so that he might be just and the justifier of the one who has faith in Jesus."

Romans 6:3-4 "Do you not know that all of us who have been baptized into Christ Jesus were baptized into his death? We were buried therefore with him by baptism into death, in order that, just as Christ was raised from the dead by the glory of the Father, we too might walk in newness of life."

In these example passages, Paul is saying that, not only does one need to repent of ones sins and turn back to God, but one must also have faith in the crucifixion of Christ to be saved. Here is a jump from personal repentance to human sacrifice. Where in the Torah (Law) in the existing Hebrew Scriptures does God ever demand faith in a bloody human sacrifice for the forgiveness and remission of sins? In fact, there is no such law or command. However, such stories do exist in Mystery Religions which were popular in the Roman Empire at the time. In fact, one such religion existed in Galilee and is mentioned in the Hebrew Scriptures in the Eighth chapter of the Book of Ezekiel:

"In the sixth year, in the sixth month, on the fifth day of the month, as I sat in my house, with the elders of Judah sitting before me, the hand of the Lord GOD fell upon me there. Then I looked, and behold, a form that had the appearance of a man[6]. Below what appeared to be his waist was fire,

---

4   or brothers and sisters

5   2:1 some manuscripts mystery (or secret)

6   8:2 By revocalization (compare Septuagint); Hebrew *of fire*

and above his waist was something like the appearance of brightness, like gleaming metal[7]. He put out the form of a hand and took me by a lock of my head, and the Spirit lifted me up between earth and heaven and brought me in visions of God to Jerusalem, to the entrance of the gateway of the inner court that faces north, where was the seat of the image of jealousy, which provokes to jealousy. And behold, the glory of the God of Israel was there, like the vision that I saw in the valley.

Then he said to me, "Son of man, lift up your eyes now toward the north." So I lifted up my eyes toward the north, and behold, north of the altar gate, in the entrance, was this image of jealousy. And he said to me, "Son of man, do you see what they are doing, the great abominations that the house of Israel are committing here, to drive me far from my sanctuary? But you will see still greater abominations."

"And he brought me to the entrance of the court, and when I looked, behold, there was a hole in the wall. Then he said to me, 'Son of man, dig in the wall.' So I dug in the wall, and behold, there was an entrance. And he said to me, 'Go in, and see the vile abominations that they are committing here.' So I went in and saw. And there, engraved on the wall all around, was every form of creeping things and loathsome beasts, and all the idols of the house of Israel. And before them stood seventy men of the elders of the house of Israel, with Jaazaniah the son of Shaphan standing among them. Each had his censer in his hand, and the smoke of the cloud of incense went up. Then he said to me, 'Son of man, have you seen what the elders of the house of Israel are doing in the dark, each in his room of pictures? For they say, The LORD does not see us, the LORD has forsaken the land.' He said also to me, 'You will see still greater abominations that they commit.'

"Then he brought me to the entrance of the north gate of the house of the LORD, and behold, there sat women weeping for Tammuz. Then he said to me, 'Have you seen this, O son of man? You will see still greater abominations than these.'

"And he brought me into the inner court of the house of the LORD. And behold, at the entrance of the temple of the LORD, between the porch and the altar, were about twenty-five men, with their backs to the temple of the LORD, and their faces toward the east, worshiping the sun toward the east. Then he said to me, 'Have you seen this, O son of man? Is it too light a thing for the house of Judah to commit the abominations that they commit here, that they should fill the land with violence and provoke me still further to anger?

---

[7]   8:2 Or *amber*

Behold, they put the branch to their nose[8]. Therefore I will act in wrath. My eye will not spare, nor will I have pity. And though they cry in my ears with a loud voice, I will not hear them.'

Tammuz was a suffering God-man whose death was celebrated each spring in Galilee, Lebanon and Syria. Here we have the LORD showing Ezekiel that the rites of Tammuz were actually being practiced secretly within the Temple in Jerusalem, and the LORD considers such practice to be an abomination. But this is not what Paul has to say about Jesus Christ (PBUH). Paul states the following:

Colossians 2:1-15 "For I want you to know how great a struggle I have for you and for those at Laodicea and for all who have not seen me face to face, that their hearts may be encouraged, being knit together in love, to reach all the riches of full assurance of understanding and the knowledge of God's mystery, which is Christ, in whom are hidden all the treasures of wisdom and knowledge. I say this in order that no one may delude you with plausible arguments. For though I am absent in body, yet I am with you in spirit, rejoicing to see your good order and the firmness of your faith in Christ.

See to it that no one takes you captive by philosophy and empty deceit, according to human tradition, according to the elemental spirits[9] of the world, and not according to Christ. For in him the whole fullness of deity dwells bodily, and you have been filled in him, who is the head of all rule and authority. In him also you were circumcised with a circumcision made without hands, by putting off the body of the flesh, by the circumcision of Christ, having been buried with him in baptism, in which you were also raised with him through faith in the powerful working of God, who raised him from the dead. And you, who were dead in your trespasses and the uncircumcision of your flesh, God made alive together with him, having forgiven us all our trespasses, by canceling the record of debt that stood against us with its legal demands. This he set aside, nailing it to the cross. He disarmed the rulers and authorities[10] and put them to open shame, by triumphing over them in him[11]."

In this passage, Paul even calls Christ "God's Mystery." Paul states that the fullness of deity dwells bodily in Christ, Deity and humanity together (a God-man, so to speak). The King James Translation has 'Godhead' instead

---

[8]   8:17 Or *my*

[9]   2:8 Or elementary principles; also verse 20

[10]   2:15 Probably demonic rulers and authorities

[11]   2:15 Or in it (that is, the cross)

of 'Deity.' Is Paul merely stating in mystical terms that God's Word and Holy Spirit (which are not persons) are both present in Christ? Or, rather, is Paul making the claim that Jesus Christ is the Incarnation of God? Trinitarians and Modalistic Monarchians believe Paul is saying that Jesus Christ is the Incarnation, thus, God becomes a man and dies as a ransom for sin. Believers are to be 'crucified with Christ,' 'baptized into Christ's death,' and rise from the dead by faith in the Resurrection when coming out of the water. This does make Paul's baptism appear to be an initiation rite similar to those in other Mystery Religions, where the believer benefits in some way from the death of the God-man.

Since the first of the Ten Commandments teaches one shall not have any strange gods besides God (Jehovah), the only way out for early Christian scholars who were trying to make sense of these passages, which were believed to be infallible scriptures, was to somehow describe One God as a unity of Divine Persons. The Son cannot be a god beside God, thus, together, the Father and Son (and Holy Spirit, as per the baptismal formula in Chapter Eight of Matthew's Gospel) must be either divine persons in the Godhead, or divine Modes within the Godhead, as the Modalistic Monarchians believed.

Thus, even if Paul of Tarsus was not a Trinitarian, or did not believe Jesus Christ (PBUH) was the incarnation of God, what he wrote about God and Christ might be taken this way in order to avoid outright Polytheism.

Lastly, it should be noted that God, for the Trinitarian Christian, is the eternal 'What,' not the eternal 'Who.' If God is a Trinity consisting of three distinct 'Coeternals (i.e. Three Coeternal Persons),' and in Western Christianity 'Coequals (or Coeternal Persons),' then God is Unity of Persons, not a Person. A 'Unity' is a 'What.' A 'Person' is a 'Who.'

APPENDIX II.
The Various Theories of the Atonement of Christ in Christian History.

The central doctrine of the majority or Pauline Christianity is, without a doubt, the sacrifice of Christ, who made atonement for sin. A survey of popular hymns sung in churches every Sunday in England and the USA from the last few centuries will demonstrate this proposition.

"There is a fountain filled with blood
Drawn from Immanuel's veins,
And sinners washed beneath that flood
Lose all their guilty stains."

– From: There is a Fountain, words by William Cooper (1731 C.E. – 1800 C.E.)

Mercy there was grace, and grace was free;
Pardon there was multiplied to me;
There my wounded soul found liberty
At Calvary!

– At Calvary 1895 C.E., words by William Newell, music by Daniel Brink Towner

Alas, and did my Savior bleed,
And did my Sovereign die?
Would He devote that sacred head
For such a worm as I?

– Alas and Did My Savior Bleed, words by Isaac Watts (1674 C.E. – 1748 C.E.)

We can see from these words what the majority of Protestant Evangelical Christians have believed since the Reformation: Humans are guilty sinners before God, with wounded souls and therefore are worms that require the death of a Savior/Sovereign (indeed, a suffering God-man) so that they can be washed in His blood in order to have the stain of sin washed away, and be freely pardoned by the mercy and grace of God in order to gain liberty.

Have all Christians at all times believed exactly this view of the Atonement of Christ? The answer, of course, is no. Below is a short overview of the theories of the Atonement of Christ. Five books were consulted to prepare this overview. They are:

i. Systematic Theology by Louis Berkhof – Published 1932, revised 1938.

ii. The History of Christian Doctrines by Louis Berkhof – published 1937.

iii. Systematic Theology by John Miley – published 1892.

iv. The Kindness of God Our Savior by Gordon C. Olson – published 1962.

v. Christus Victor: A Historical Study of the Three Main Types of the Idea of the Atonement by Gustav Aulen – published 1931.

I choose these works because they are familiar to me and representative of different schools of thought. Louis Berkhof (1873 C.E. – 1957 C.E.) was a well-known Netherlands-born conservative and orthodox Reformed theologian. John Miley (1813 C.E. – 1895 C.E.) was a well-known Methodist theologian of the 19th Century C.E. who wrote "The Atonement of Christ" in 1879 C.E. In this book, Miley defended the Governmental view of the atonement which had been heavily influenced by the writings of Hugo Grotius, a student of Jacob Arminius and a scholar of international law whose writings are still consulted today. Gustav Aulen was a Lutheran theologian from Sweden who championed a view of the atonement believed by early Christian writers. Gordon C. Olson was an obscure and somewhat controversial 20th Century C.E. theologian whose writings on the atonement (and especially the Governmental theory) introduced me to various historical theories of the atonement.

First, I'll briefly discuss what John Miley wrote about the atonement. Miley saw twenty-one major historic theories of the atonement up to the time of his writing (c. 1879 C.E.). Miley grouped these theories into five main views of the atonement. Gordon C. Olson, like Miley, supported the Governmental theory of the atonement and saw more or less the same five main views of the atonement as Miley, but combines two of the views so that Olson lists four main views of the atonement. In Appendix B of Olson's book, The Kindness of God Our Savior, a brief description of these groups of theories is given.

I will give an outline of them below, with comments from the other scholars whose books I mentioned above:

1. The Satisfaction Theory – strictly vicarious and exactly equivalent to man's guilt

    i.   Satisfaction to Satan, to whom man had given his allegiance and must be liberated by Christ paying to him the ransom price – common in the 3rd through 11th centuries.

       Historic Christians who held this view:

- Irenaeus (2nd century C.E.)

- Origen (3rd century C.E.)

- Gregory of Nyssa (4th century C.E.)

- Augustine of Hippo (late 4th to early 5th centuries C.E.)

    ii. Satisfaction to the Father universally for all mankind through the sacrificial death of the Divine Logos who became one with lost humanity – this was the view of Athanasius of Alexandria, the great defender of the Trinity and deity of Christ at Nicaea I 325 C.E. In salvation the goodness of God must act consistent with His truthfulness and honor, which involves the principle of justice. Man must be freed not only from the penalty of sin, but from sin itself and quickened unto life.

    iii. Satisfaction to the ethical nature of God, which demands absolute legal vindication – this is the view of Anselm of Canterbury (1033 C.E. – 1109 C.E.), the famous Scholastic churchman, as described in his book "Cur Deus Homo" (or "Why the God-man?") written 1098 C.E., and considered by many to be the first scientific treatise on the atonement. Gustav Aulen wrote that is the Roman Catholic teaching on penance applied to the atonement. God's honor and supremacy has been offended by mankind who has incurred a debt to God which can only be paid by punishment, or by some substituted sacrifice. The sacrifice by the God-man, Jesus Christ, in obedience, suffering, and death, acquired merit before God and which may be imputed to the believer as a perfect judicial standing. Berkhof criticizes those opponents of Anselm who call this view the commercial view of the atonement and states that Anselm's theory is not identical to the view of the majority of Protestant Reformers, although Anselm's view was a major influence on the Reformed view. Many see the Roman

Catholic sacrament of Penance as an influence on Anselm's view of the Atonement.

iv. Satisfaction through a mystical union or a sacrificial bearing of the penalty of sin, providing a relative satisfaction as opposed to an absolute and strictly legal satisfaction in the full discharge of guilt. This is the view of Bernard of Clairvaux (b. 1091 C.E. – d. 1153 C.E.) in response to Anselm. Bernard was considered a pious and influential monk in his time.

v. Satisfaction to the offended holiness and justice of God through Christ's bearing the full penalty of sin in His vicarious death. Olson says this is the view of the early Protestant Reformers Martin Luther and John Calvin (early-mid 16th Century C.E.) and most other Reformers of the time, who adopted Anselm's principle of strict judicial satisfaction. The entire guilt and punishment that sinners deserve is transferred to Christ on the cross. Thus, sin and guilt may no longer be imputed to those Elect for whom Christ died, forever.

vi. As aforementioned, except with greater emphasis in the early Post-Reformation period upon the active righteousness of Christ being imputed to the believer as a perfect positive standing. This is seen in Lutheran and Reformed confessions, and in the Federal Headship Theory of Coccecius (1603 C.E. – 1669 C.E.) and more fully elaborated upon in the writings of Turretin (1663 C.E. – 1687 C.E.). In this view, under the covenant of works, Adam's sin is imputed to all because Adam is the federal head of the human race. Augustine of Hippo (354 C.E. – 450 C.E.) had postulated an organic or natural headship of Adam. Thus, through the covenant of Grace, Jesus Christ becomes the Federal Head of all who actually experience salvation (the Elect). This means that the guilt of sin for the Elect is literally discharged before the sin is actually committed, because it is discharged when Jesus Christ says "It is finished!" before his death on the cross at Calvary.

2. The Governmental Theory – The Atonement was necessary to solve problems of God as a Moral Governor, who lovingly desires to reconcile man.

i. The sufferings of Christ were necessary to the Divine government, rather than to the Divine nature – Gregory of Nazianzus. Olson appears to attribute the seeds of the Governmental view to Gregory of Nazianzus (330 C.E. – 390 C.E.). Gregory strongly opposed the idea of a ransom paid to Satan, but could not understand why a ransom should be paid to the Father. Gregory could only fall back on the economy of God and therefore put forth no theory of satisfaction. Other writers, such as Athanasius, also mentioned God's governmental problems.

ii. Christ suffered unto death in His human nature, and not in His Divine nature, and thus the Atonement was not of infinite value to pay fully for the eternal punishment of sinners, but was graciously accepted by God the Father as sufficient to satisfy Divine Justice – Duns Scotus. Olson attributes the next step toward the development of the Government theory to Duns Scotus (1265 C.E. – 1308 C.E.) who was a Roman Catholic philosopher of the scholastic school. Scotus' view of the atonement is a response to Anselm's theory of the atonement.

iii. Christ, 'the Savior of the World,' died for all men and every man, and His grace is extended to all. His atoning sacrifice is in and of itself sufficient for the redemption of the whole world, and is intended for all by God the Father. The sacrifice of Christ is not the payment of a debt, nor is it a complete satisfaction of justice for sin. It is a divinely appointed condition which precedes the forgiveness of sin, just as the death of a lamb or a goat in the Mosaic economy. Christ's suffering took the place of a penalty, so that His sufferings have the same effect in reconciling God to man, and procuring the forgiveness of sin, that the sinner's endurance of the punishment due to his sins would have had. The sufferings of Christ were not a substituted penalty, but a substitute for the penalty. This is the view of Jacob (James) Arminius (1560 C.E. – 1609 C.E.) and many of his students, including Episcopus (1583 C.E. – 1643 C.E.). This view would have a major influence upon the Methodists.

iv. God is a benevolent ruler exercising control over moral beings by good and wise laws designed for the mutual happiness of Him and them. Regulation in a moral government is by means of promised blessings for conformity and penalties of suffering for disobedience. While God in compassionate mercy is willing to forgive or relax His just claims against rebellious moral beings upon evidence of a willingness to cease from rebellion and return to happy submission, He cannot wisely do so without a terrible measure of enlightenment and suffering by a Being of profound dignity. This must demonstrate before all the dreadful nature and consequences of sin and provide an eternal moral force against further indulgence and heartbreak to Him as well as to them. This is the view of Hugo Grotius (1563 C.E.

– 1645 C.E.), a prominent Dutch jurist whose works on international law are still in use today. Grotius was a student of Jacob Arminius and wrote a book against the Socinians in 1617 C.E.

v.   The sufferings and especially the death of Christ were sacrificial, were not the punishment of the law but were equivalent in meaning to it, were representative of it and substituted for it. The demands of the law were not satisfied by the sacrifice, but the honor of the law was promoted by it as much as the honor would have been promoted by inflicting the legal penalty upon all sinners. The distributive (or vindictive) justice of God was not satisfied by it, but His general justice (or justice for the public good) as a responsible Moral Governor was perfectly satisfied. The active obedience or Holiness of Christ made possible his virtuous death in man's behalf, but is not legally imputed to the believer. Christ's atonement was made for all men in the same sense. It was necessary on God's account to enable Him as a consistent Ruler to fulfill His moral obligations to His subjects, when repentant sinners are pardoned through a commitment of faith. – This is quoted from E. A. Park, 1883 C.E., who was a professor at Andover Theological Seminary which was founded by Dr. Timothy Dwight in 1807 C.E. Dwight was the son-in-law of Jonathan Edwards (1703 C.E. – 1758 C.E.). This was the New England/New School view of the atonement (the fullest development of the Governmental Theory of the Atonement) also taught by Edwards, his son, (1745 C.E. – 1801 C.E.), Nathaniel Emmons (1745 C.E. – 1840 C.E.), Caleb Burge (1782 C.E. – 1838 C.E.), Nathaniel W. Taylor (1786 C.E. – 1858 C.E.) and Charles Grandison Finney (1792 C.E. – 1875 C.E.).

3. The Moral Influence Theory – A manifestation of suffering Divine love was necessary to subdue man's rebellion so reconciliation could take place.

There is no need to satisfy retributive justice, as in the view of Anselm and the Reformers. Nor is there a need to satisfy public justice to uphold moral government. The life and sufferings of the God-man were intended to exert a moral impression upon a hard an impenitent heart which thereby melted into contrition, and then received into favor by the boundless compassion of God (from Abelard's description). Olson attributed this view to Clement of Alexandria (about 185 C.E. – 254 C.E.), Peter Abelard (1079 C.E. – 1142 C.E.), of France who opposed Anselm; also, Horace Bushnell (1802 C.E. – 1876 C.E.), a lawyer and New England Pastor. Many liberal theologians of the late 19th and 20th centuries C.E. accepted the views of Bushnell without sharing his deep sincerity.

Many theologians who hold to the Governmental view of the atonement do not deny the moral influence of the sacrifice of Christ, but a moral influence is not atonement for sin.

4. The Ethical Example Theory – Sinful man has been misguided and a noble virtuous example to challenge him to a new way of living.

If man is to realize his potential and be reconciled to God, he must repent and reform his ways. For this purpose Jesus Christ was miraculously brought into this world and thus was not a mere man (as believed by the Socinians in the 1600s C.E.), or was natural born and a religious Genius who identified himself with God in special devotion to achieve a unique ministry to mankind (as believed by Unitarians in the 1700s). The Ethical Example Theory was developed by Laelius Socinus (1525 C.E. – 1562 C.E.) and his nephew Faustus Socinus (1539 C.E. – 1604 C.E.) in Poland. Unitarians who trace their views back to Arius (256 C.E. – 336 C.E.), and others who believe Christ was a mere man hold this view.

Berkhof, in "The History of Christian Doctrine," describes the history of the atonement in a way not too dissimilar to Gordon C. Olson, excerpt that Berkhof states that the view of the atonement as developed by the Calvinist Reformers is the correct view. Berkhof begins by describing pre-Anselm views of the atonement in terms of Greek and Latin Patristic Theology. Berkhof also discussed the Mystical View of the atonement as advanced by liberal theologians whose writings were not available for Miley's Systematic Theology.

Aulen, in his book Christus Victor: A Historical Study of the Three Main Types of the Idea of Atonement, groups the various theories of the atonement into three categories, the classic Christus Victor view, the Satisfaction view of Anselm, and the Moral Influence view of Peter Abelard. The Christus Victor view is described in the writings of the early Church Father Irenaeus, and also in the writings of some early Fathers who came after Irenaeus. Aulen believes the only authentic view of the atonement is the Christus Victor view. Aulen believes this is the same view of the atonement Martin Luther came to believe. Some Lutherans do agree with Aulen on this point. The Christus Victor view of the atonement is essentially the same view held by the Eastern Orthodox churches. In the Christus Victor view, Christ does battle against Satan, and other evil cosmic forces (tyrants) to which man is in bondage, and triumphs over all of these enemies. In doing so, God reconciles the world to himself. Aulen considers the other two categories as later speculations that are not authentic.

APPENDIX III.
Indices of the Introduction

1. Glossary

Allah: The name of God in Arabic. The equivalent in Hebrew is "Eloah," while the equivalent in Aramaic is "Alahah." Allah may be a contraction of the words "al-ilah" or "the god" in Arabic. Some fundamentalist evangelical Christians wrongly refer to Allah as the Moon God of the Arabs. Rather, Allat was a feminine deity identified with polytheistic Arab moon Goddess. Many Eurasian cultures worshipped a moon goddess, such as Roman goddess Luna or the Greek goddess Selene.

Abu: Arabic word that means "father of," similar to Aramaic "Abba."

Ahmadiyyah: An originally pro-British sect based on the teachings of Ghulam Ahmad who eventually declared himself the "Mahdi" promised messiah and reformer of the Muslims. One subsect of this sect believes one must accept Ghulam Ahmad as the Mahdi to be a Muslim, while the majority believes that one does not have to accept Ghulam Ahmad to be a Muslim. It is considered a heretical sect by most Sunni and Shia Muslims.

Annulment: A legal procedure in the Roman Catholic Church for declaring a marriage as null and void, as if it never had been performed. Eastern Orthodox Churches have Church Divorces instead of annulments.

Archbishop: An honorary title for a bishop which has pastoral authority over several dioceses which are each ruled by bishops. The diocese overseen by an archbishop is called by the honorary title of archdiocese.

Arminian: The name given to the followers of Dutch Theologian Jacob Arminius who disagreed with some of the teachings of John Calvin.

Arminianism: An adherent to the teachings of Jacob Arminius and/or his followers.

Assembly of God: A Pentecostal Christian denomination that formed in the early 20th century near the beginning of the Pentecostal Movement.

Baptist Church: A group of Christian denominations which usually have a Congregational form of local church government, and baptize adults believers only.

Bishop: from the Greek "Episcopus" which means "overseer." An ordained clergyman who is higher than a priest and oversees a diocese, which is made up of a number of parishes. Priests may perform all sacraments except Confirmation / Chrismation and Holy Orders (ordination of priests and bishops), which may only be performed by the bishop.

Born Again: Also Born From Above, the term used by many Evangelical Christians to define the regeneration experience at initial salvation. In John Gospel, chapter 3, it is reported that Jesus Christ declared to a Pharisee named Nicodemus that one cannot see the Kingdom of God unless one is Born Again.

Caliph: Arabic word meaning "successor," as in the leader that succeeds as the leader of the Muslims after Prophet Muhammad (PBUH). Sunni Muslims believe Abu Bakr was rightly elected as the first Caliph. Shia Muslims believe Ali Ibn Abu Talib (PBUH) was supposed to be the first Caliph, and cite traditions considered authentic by Sunni Muslims to advance their case.

Caliphate: The officer of the succssorship, the station of commander of the Faithful (Muslims) after the Prophet Muhammad (PBUH).

Calvinism: The name later given to 5 particular points of doctrine in Reformed Christianity as defined in opposition to Arminians in the early 17th century. Named after the French Protestant Reformer and Theologian John Calvin.

Calvinist: An adherent to the 5 points of Calvinism.

Canon: A rule.

Canon Law: From the Greel word "kanon" which means "rule," is the Rule of Law. Roman Catholic Canon Law differs from Anglican Canon Law, which differs again from Eastern Orthodox Canon Law.

Catechism: From the Greek "catechismos" which is a manual of doctrine, usually but not always in question and answer form, and sometimes with scripture proofs, used to teach adherents the basic beliefs and practices of the Church. This form has been in use since ancient times by Christians.

Chalcedon: The location of the 4th Ecumenical Council of the Catholic Church, held in 451 C.E., which defines the nature of Jesus Christ as being fully God and fully man, with two natures (one divine, one human) and two wills (again, one divine and one human).

Christology: The branch of theology that deals with the nature of Jesus Christ.

Commentator: After Vatican II, a layman who makes announcements and may be a reader of epistles during the Mass.

Council of Trent: The 19th Ecumenical Council of the Roman Catholic Church, which was held from December 1545 C.E. to December 1563 C.E., in the city of Trent within the Holy Roman Empire. This council was in part a response to the Protestant Reformation, and addressed the need for major reform in the Church. The Seven Sacraments were definitively described, and the Deuterocanonical Books of the Bible were declared to have full canonicity, which led to their total rejection by most Protestants.

Creed: From the Latin word "credo" which means "I believe," a statement of belief, sometimes called a "symbol," usually of a religious nature.

Crucifixion: A form of execution used by the Ancient Roman Empire and other peoples, whereby the victim is hung on a pole, tree, or wooden cross in such a way that it is difficult for the victim to breathe. It is reported that a healthy young man might hang in this way for several days before dying of suffocation. The New Testament reports that Jesus Christ was crucified on a "stauros," the Greek word for pole or stake. Crucifixion is from two Latin words which mean "to fix to a cross."

Discipleship Class: Also, a New Members class or a Catechism Class, where new Christians or Christians new to a particular denomination are taught basic Christian doctrines and practices.

Divine Liturgy: The Liturgy used by various Roman Catholic, Eastern Orthodox, and other Catholic Churches to celebrate the Holy Eucharist on Sundays and other days. The Greek and Russian Orthodox use the Divine Liturgy of St. John Chrysostom and St. Basil the Great. Until just after the Vatican II Ecumenical Council, the Traditional Mass was in use by the Western Rite of the Roman Catholic Church.

Dogma: From the Greek word which means "that which seems to one opinion of belief." Dogmas are the central doctrines that must be believed by all members of a particular church.

Eastern Orthodox Church: Those Eastern Catholics which remained in fellowship with the Partriarch of Constaninople after the Papal Legate Cardinal Humbert excommunicated the Patriarch of Constantinople in 1054 C.E., who in turn excommunicated the Pope, the Bishop of Rome.

Ebionites: Very early Jewish Christian sect which believed Jesus Christ is the promised Messiah and Prophet. Most Ebionites did not believe in the Virgin Birth but rather believed Jesus Christ was a man, the son of two righteous Jewish parents. Although they believed Jesus Christ was murdered because of his preaching, the Ebionites believed salvation was the result of following the teaching and examples of Jesus Christ. The Ebionites rejected Paul of Tarsus as a false Messiah. Some later held to Gnostic teachings.

Ecumenical Council: An important meeting of all Catholic Bishops to solve problems that arise in the Catholic Church. Roman Catholics recognize 21 Ecumenical Councils. Eastern Orthodoxy only recognizes 7 Ecumenical Councils.

Evangelical: A proponent of Evangelicalism, which stresses personal faith and Biblical authority.

Five Pillars: The traditional belief and practice of Sunni Muslims: 1) Shahada or Creed, 2) Salat (5 Daily Prayers), 3) Sadaqah or Charity Tax, 4) Sawm or Fasting, 5) Hajj or Pilgrimage

Five Roots: "12er" Shia Muslims define ideology before practice. Thus, rather than the 5 Traditional Sunni Pillars, 12er Shia Muslims define the Five Roots of Religion as follows: 1) Tawheed or Oneness of God, 2) Justice of God, 3) Prophethood, 4) Guidance or Imamate, 5) Resurrection. A second list, the Ten Branches of Religion, define the practices of 12er Shia Muslims.

Fundamentalist: A proponent of Fundamentalism, which includes strong faith and strict adherence to the basic doctrines of one form of "Biblical" Christianity. The five basic principles of the Fundamentalist movement among Evangelicals in the early 20th century were: 1) The inspiration and inerrancy of the Bible, 2) The Virgin birth of Jesus Christ (PBUH), 3) The Crucifixion of Christ as an atonement for sin, 4) The bodily resurrection of Jesus Christ (PBUH), 5) Jesus Christ perfomed real miracles. Fundamentalism was a reaction to the Modernist movement within Christianity.

Gnostic: One who knows, from the Greek word "gnosis" which means "knowledge." Early Christian Gnostics believed they had secret knowledge given by Jesus Christ (PBUH) that proto-Orthodox (early Catholic) Christians did not possess.

Gnosticism: A movement that believes it has secret knowledge, often applied to Christian Gnostics in early Christianity.

Godfather/Godmother: In the Roman Catholic Church, a catholic man and woman in good standing with the Church who sponsors a child for the Sacrament of Baptism and makes the vows for the child.

Hadeeth: Arabic for "Sayings/Traditions of the Prophet."

Halal: Food that Muslims is allowed to eat. 12er Shia Muslims and many Sunni Muslims believe a clean animal according to the Quran must be slaughtered by a Muslim of sound mind according to certain rules in order to be Halal or allowed to eat. Also, any allowed practice according to various schools of Muslim jurisprudence is considered 'Halal.'

Hijab: Head covering worn by Muslim women according to Muslim laws and the Quran.

Ibn: or "Bin" are Arabic words that mean "son," similar to the Hebrew "ben."

Icon: A painted picture that has been painted according to church rules and blessed by a priest. Icons are used by all branches of Catholics but are more popular among Eastern Catholic and Eastern Orthodox Churches, which do not usually use statues which are common in the Western Roman Catholic Church. They are sometimes called "windows into Heaven."

Imam: In Sunni Islam, the leader of a mosque, or an important leader in a period of time. In Shia Islam, the Imam is an infallible guide who interprets the scripture after the Messenger is off the scene. The largest group of Shia Muslims, the 12er Shia Muslims, believe there have been 12 Imams since the passing of Prophet Muhammad (PBUH). The 12th Imam, Al-Mahdi (PBUH), is now hidden from physical view (occultation) but will return in the future along with Jesus Christ (PBUH).

Jefferson Bible: A compilation of New Testament passages edited by American President Thomas Jefferson which agreed with his Unitarian/Deist Faith. The Jefferson Bible makes no mention of the New Testament passage that deal with the Virgin Birth, miracles, and Resurrection. Jesus is portrayed as a good and wise and compassionate man whose example and teachings are great. Jesus is finally murdered by his enemies and buried, living only through his teachings.

Judaism: The religion of the Jews. Several sects existed within Judaism in the 1st Century C.E.

Khoja: A term used for a merchant class of Hindus as well as Shia Muslims who converted from Hinduism in the 19th Century C.E.

Kosher: Food that a practicing adherent to Judaism may eat. This food is considered clean by the Torah and also blessed by a Rabbi.

Lord: In Trinitarian and Oneness Christianity, Lord can refer to God, or to Jesus Christ. LORD, when all capitals in the King James Translation, refers to the Hebrew word Yahweh or Jehovah, "I AM THAT I AM," the name for God in the Hebrew Scriptures.

Manicheans: Followers of Mani, a 3rd Century C.E. Iranian who believed he was the promised Paraclete described in the Gospel of John chapters 14 through 16. Manichaeism contained elements of Judaism, Christian Gnosticism, Christianity, Buddhism, and Zoroastrianism, and Mani claimed to be the Last Prophet or Seal of the Prophets. A missionary religion, Manichaeism competed with Christianity and Zoroastrianism, and in the 3rd century claimed followers from the Western Roman Empire to China. Mani, who was related to the Parthian Royal House through his mother Mariam, was executed when he fell out favor with the Parthian government. The Roman Catholic St. Augustine of Hippo had been a Manichaean for 9 years before converting to Christianity. The Medieval Cathari and Bogomils were examples of Neo-Manichaean thought in Europe. In China, there were Manichaeans until the just before the 16th Century C.E.

Mass: The Roman Catholic Divine Liturgy in the Western Rite, where the consecrated Bread and Wine is served as the Body and Blood of Christ to communicants.

Mecca: The Arabian city where the Kaaba, the House of God that Abraham (PBUH) built for Ishmael (PBUH) and his descendants stands. Later descendants of Ishmael (PBUH) filled the Kaaba with idols.

Medina: Formerly known as Yathraib, Medinat Al-Nabi (the City of the Prophet), or Medina for short, was the first city in Arabia to accept the leadership of Prophet Muhammad (PBUH) and the site of the first Islamic State,

Methodist: A holiness movement that began in the Anglican Church as the Holy Club at Oxford University in England. Members of this Holy Club included John Wesley, who would become an Anglican priest, his brother Charles Wesley, who composed many hymns, and George Whitefield, who also was ordained an Anglican priest. Wesley and Whitfield both preached open-air revival meetings. Wesley's theology was Arminian (see entry), while Whitfield was a Calvinist (see entry on Calvinism). The Methodist movement was also involved in many social justice issues of the time. The Methodist Church came into being when John Wesley could not find an Anglican Bishop to ordain other leaders in his movement as priests. Wesley, only a priest, ordained Dr. Thomas Coke, an Anglican Priest, as a bishop. Coke then ordained other men as priests and bishops. This was strenuously opposed by Wesley's brother Charles, and others.

Montanism: A movement in Christianity led by Montanus (early 2nd Century C.E.) which was a reaction to the "laxness" that was seen in the Church. Montanist, a convert to Christianity, believed he was the promised Paraclete described in The Gospel of John chapters 14 through 16. Anyone who disagreed with his prophecies he considered to have sinned against the Holy Spirit. Montanus predicted the Second Coming of Christ would happen soon in his home town in Asia Minor. After his death, the movement stressed the reaction against laxness in the Church and de-emphasized the prophetic nature of the movement. The late 2nd Century C.E. Latin Church Father Tertullian became a Montanist until late in life, when he left the movement to begin his own group.

Montanist: An adherent to Montanism.

Muslim: Someone who is a Submitter unto God according to Islam. (Arabic = submitter). Islam is Submission (Arabic) unto God. The Arabic "slm" root is the same as the Hebrew "slm" root from where we get the Arabic word "Salam" and the Hebrew word "Shalom," which mean "Peace."

Mutazilites: Rationalist Muslims of the classic period. They were neutral in the controversy between Sunni Muslims and Shia Muslims, but considered Ali Ibn Abu Talib (PBUH), the first Imam of Shia Muslims, as the best companion of the Prophet. A classic Mutazilite scholar wrote a commentary on the Nahjul Balagha that is still studied by 12er Shia Muslim scholars today.

Nag Hammadi: The location in Egypt where a large Gnostic documents written in the Coptic Language but using the Greek Alphabet was discovered in December 1945. These documents date to the middle-to late 4th century C.E. Many scholars believe that these scrolls were hidden after Bishop Athanasius wrote a pastoral letter in 363 C.E. which gives the same list of 27 books that included in the Catholic New Testament.

Nahjul Balagha: In English, the Peak of Eloquence. This is a selection of Sermon excerpts, letters, and wisdom sayings of Imam Ali Ibn Abu Talib (PBUH), the first Imam of all Shia Muslim sects, who was the cousin of Prophet Muhammad (PBUH) and husband to the Prophets daughter Sayida Fatima Al-Zahraa (PBUH). This book is considered the most important book of authentic traditions by Shia Muslims. Many Sunni Muslims and Sufis hold this book in high regard.

Nation of Islam: An African American Separatist sect of Muslims founded by Elijah Muhammad. Recently, the Nation of Islam has begun to move closer to position of Sunni Muslims on its outlook of Islam.

Nazoreans: Several sects of Torah observant Christians in the very early Church. This is the name used by the followers of Jesus Christ before they were called Christians according to the New Testament. Some Nazoreans held Gnostic beliefs. Most believed in the virgin birth. Nazoreans and Ebionites lived in similar areas. The Nazoreans tolerated Paul but did not take teachings from him.

New Testament: The 27 Books of the 2nd part of the Christian Bible. Although most of the books were used by all Catholic Christians by the end of the 2nd Century C.E., the final list of New Testament was officially decided by the Western Church in 397 C.E. and the whole Catholic Church in 430 C.E.

Nicene Creed: Also Nicene-Constantinopolitan Creed, the official state sponsored creed of the Catholic Church, which was defined by Catholic Bishops at the first two Ecumenical Church Councils. These were the Council of Nicaea I in 325 C.E. and the Council of Constantinople I in 381 C.E. The Nicene Creed defines the Catholic view of God as a unity of three co-eternal persons, the Father, Son, and Holy Spirit, one essence in three substances. This creed also defines the "four marks of the Church" i.e. One, Holy, Catholic (universal) and Apostolic. One Baptism is applied for the forgiveness of sins. The Resurrection of the Dead and life in the New World which comes after the Resurrection are also declared.

Parish: Traditionally, an area of land where the Catholic Christians residing on the land attend a particular church and receive sacraments from the clergy at that church. Several parishes make up a diocese, which is governed by a bishop.

Pastor: From the Latin word for "shepherd," a pastor would be a priest or a bishop in the Roman Catholic and Eastern Orthodox Churches. The pastor may be the elder or an elder in a Protestant Church, or may be a position for pastoral care of church members who is hired and fulfills the duties of his office an answers to the deacon board.

Pauline Epistles: A library of letters in the New Testament, most or all of which were written by Paul of Tarsus.

Pentecostals: Evangelical Christians who believe the Baptism of the Holy Spirit described in the Second Chapter of The Acts of the Apostles is a separate, second experience of Grace after the Born Again experience. Some Pentecostals even believe one cannot be saved unless one is baptized in the Holy Spirit.

Pope: The Supreme Pontiff (or Holy Father) of the Roman Catholic Church: who rules Vatican City.

Priest: From the Greek word "Presbyteros" which means "elder." In the Roman Catholic and Eastern Orthodox Churches, an ordained priest may perform the sacraments of Baptism, Holy Communion, Penance, Matrimony, and the Sacrament of the Sick.

Prophet: According to Sunni Muslims, one who is sent by God to teach his people. According to Shia Islam, a Prophet is an infallible teacher to his peoples. Both Sunni and Shia Muslims believe that Prophets may also be Messengers, i.e. one who brings a scripture to his people.

Protestant: Historically, one who "protested" against the perceived errors of the Roman Catholic Church. See the entry on Reformation.

Proto-Orthodox: A name used by New Testament scholar Bart Ehrman and others to describe the movement of early Christianity that eventually became the Catholic Church.

Quran: The Holy Book Muslims believe was revealed through the Prophet Muhammad (PBUH).

Rapture: According to Classic Dispensationalism, the Second Coming of Jesus Christ in the first phase, where all true Christians, dead (and now resurrected) and alive, go to meet Jesus Christ in the air and are taken to heaven, and return with Christ to Earth 7 years later at the Battle of Armageddon.

Reformation: A move by Protestants to reform the Roman Catholic Church. Reform movements had been in existence for many centuries, but the Protestant Reformation was said to have begun when the German Catholic priest and theologian Martin Luther nailed the "Ninety-Five Theses on the Power and Efficacy of Indulgences" to the door of the church at Wittenburg, Germany, in 1517 C.E.

Rite: Can be a religious ceremony or can be the liturgies and religious ceremonies of a particular section of the Roman Catholic Church, such as the Maronite Rite practiced by Lebanese Catholics, or the Byzantine Rite, practiced by Byzantine (Greek) Catholics.

Roman Catholic Church: That part of the Original Catholic Church which is still in union with the Pope. There are over 2 billion Roman Catholics as of the year 2000.

Rosary: Prayer Beads. The Rosary of Mary is used in the Western Catholic Churches. Eastern Churches usually say the Jesus Prayer.

Sacraments: Also known as Holy Mysteries, these sacred rituals are thought to bestow grace from God upon Christians. Roman Catholics teach that there are Seven Sacraments. Eastern Orthodox teach there are at least Seven Sacraments. There is some difference between these churches in their description of Sacramental Theology. The Seven mutually agreed upon sacraments are: 1) Baptism, 2) Confession, 3) Holy Communion, 4) Confirmation/Chrismation, 5) Matrimony, 6) Holy Orders (ordination of deacons, priests, and bishops), and 7) The Anointing of the Sick. Lutherans have three sacraments: 1) Baptism, 2) Holy Communion, and 3) Confession. Most other Protestants teach two Sacraments: 1) Baptims, and 2) Lord's Supper (Communion). Some use the words Ordinance or Emblems instead of Sacraments.

Sahih: Arabic = Authentic, as in a Sahih Hadeeth (a tradition considered authentic by Sunni Muslims).

Scofield: C. I. Scofield propagated the Classic Dispensationalist view of Eschatology (End Times teaching) developed by Dr. John Darby in the 1820s.

Scofield also had a very popular Reference Bible with Classic Dispensationalist study notes.

Shahada: The Creed or Declaration of Faith of Muslims. "I believe that there is no God except Allah, and I believe that Muhammad is the Prophet of Allah."

Shia Muslim: A Muslim who believes the legitimate leaders of the Muslims are from the family of the Prophet Muhammad (PBUH) through Imam Ali Ibn Abu Talib (PBUH).

Sufi: One who practices the way of Sufism.

Sufism: A Mystical expression of Islam, where one works toward having a compassionate disposition by moving closer to God.

Sunni Sect: The Majority sect of Muslims. Sunnis follow the 4 Sunni Schools of Jurisprudence: 1) Hanafi, 2) Maliki, 3) Shafie, and 4) Hanbali. The name Sunni comes from the Arabic word "Sunnah" which means "the path that is walked" and refers to the ways and the manners of the Prophet Muhammad (PBUH), as recorded in the Six books of traditions (Ahadith – plural of Hadeeth) that are considered authentic by Sunnis Scholars.

Surah: A chapter in the Quran.

Systematic Theology: The study of the basic branches of theology.

Theodicy: The study of the justice of God.

Trinity: The Christian belief that God is one essence which is a unity of three co-eternal (and many would say co-equal) persons: The Father, the Son, and the Holy Spirit. The term was first used in Christian theology by Theophilus of Antioch about 172 C.E., and first used to describe the Godhead (Father, Son, and Holy Spirit) by the Latin Church Father Tertullian, in the early 3rd Century C.E.

Umayyad: The First Dynastic Caliphate, named for the Arab tribe of Umayyah. The first Caliph, Muhawiya, came to power after the murder of the 4th Caliph, Ali Ibn Abu Talib (PBUH), the first Imam according to Shia Muslims. The second Umayyad Caliph, Yazid, murdered Hussein Ibn Ali Ibn Abu Talib (PBUH), who was a grandson of the Prophet Muhammad (PBUH), and the 3rd Imam according to Shia Muslims. Yazid also murdered the male members of Hussein's family at the Battle of Karbala, located in modern day Iraq, with the exception of his son, the 4th Imam Al-Sajjad (PBUH).

Vatican II: The 21ˢᵗ Ecumenical Council of the Roman Catholic Church which was held from 1962 to 1965. Though spoken of as a Pastoral Council, many Traditional and Conservative Roman Catholics are critical of aspects of this council because they believe matters of faith and practice have been changed in the years since the Vatican II council.

.

2. Index of Names

Abu Bakr:
Lived c. 573 C.E. – 634 C.E., was an early convert to Islam and is considered one of the closest companions to the Prophet Muhammad (PBUH) by Sunni Muslims. Abu Bakr was elected as the first Caliph (successor to the Prophet) by a majority of those voting.

Al-Farabi:
Lived c. 872 C.E. – late 950 or early 951 C.E., was one of the greatest scientists in Persia and the Islamic world of his time. Farabi made contributions to the fields of logic, mathematics, medicine, music, philosophy, psychology and sociology. Farabi was an Ismaili Shia Muslim.

Ali Ibn Abi Talib:
Imam Ali Lived 598 or 600 C.E. – 561 C.E., was the cousin of Prophet Muhammad (PBUH) and husband of the Prophet's only daughter Fatima Al-Zahra. Ali Ibn Abu Talib was the 3rd Caliph, ruling the Muslim state from 556 C.E. – 561 C.E. He is known as Amir Al Mumineen (the Commander of the Faithful) and the 1st Imam of Shia Muslims. Imam Ali was the only Muslim born inside the Kaaba in Mecca and was raised in the household of the Prophet. Shia Muslims consider Ali to be the first male convert to Islam, while Sunni Muslims believe he was "among the first" converts. Very active in the service of the early Islamic state, Shia Muslims believe Imam Ali was to be the Caliph after Prophet Muhammad passed of the scene, and quote traditions considered authentic by Sunni Muslims scholars since the classic period to make their case. After the assassination of the 3rd Caliph Uthmann, Ali Ibn Abu Talib became Caliph, but encountered defiance and rebellions during his 5 year reign. Caliph Ali defeated the army of Talha, Al-Zubayr, and Aisha, one of the wives of the Prophet. Then Caliph Ali was challenged by Muhawiyah Ibn Abu Sufyan, because the latter believed the murder of his cousin Caliph Uthman was not properly avenged. Muhawiyah would become the 1st Umayyad Caliph. Settling for Arbitration with Muhawiyah rather than seeing Muslims fight Muslims, Muhawiyah gained half the kingdom from Imam Ali. A group known as the Kharijites, who was a party in Ali's coalition, opposed arbitration and broke with the coalition. Ali was murdered while praying at the mosque in Kufa, by Abd-al-Rahman Ibn Muljam, a

Kharijite, Ali Ibn Abu Talib is beloved by Sunni and Shia Muslims alike, and all but one of the classic Sufi orders trace their lineage back to Prophet Muhammad through Imam Ali ibn Abu Talib. Most Shia Muslims believe his tomb is located in the Iraqi city of Najaf.

Ambrose of Milan:
Lived c. between 337 to 341 C.E. – 397 C.E., Catholic Saint and bishop of Milan, Ambrose is considered one of the four original Doctors of the Church. He was instrumental in the conversion of Augustine of Hippo to Christianity.

Archbishop Lefebvre:
Lived 1905 C.E. – 1991 C.E., was a traditional Roman Catholic archbishop and apostolic legate who founded the Society of Saint Pius X (SSPX) in 1970 in opposition to the changes made during the Vatican II Ecumenical Council. Marcel Lefebrve was excommunicated in 1998 after ordaining four bishops without permission of Vatican. The SSPX is still the largest Traditionalist Catholic priestly society in existence.

Augustine of Hippo:
Lived 354 C.E. – 430 C.E., was a convert to Christianity from Manichaeism (although raised by a Christian mother) and later became Bishop of Hippo Rhegium in North Africa. Augustine was a philosopher and theologian influenced by the Neo-Platonic philosopher Plotinus. One of the most influential figures in Western Christianity, Augustine is considered a saint by Roman Catholics and Anglicans, and is considered by Protestants as one of the greatest influences on the Reformation. To most of the Eastern Orthodox, Augustine is considered "Blessed." The Western Christian doctrines of Original Sin and the Just War were conceived .by Augustine.

Averroes:
Lived 1126 C.E. – 1198 C.E., also known by his Arabic name Ibn Rushd, was an Andalusian-Arab Muslim. Averroes was a master of early Islamic philosophy, Islamic Theology, Jurisprudence, law, psychology, Arabic music, and the sciences of medicine, astronomy, geography, mathematics and physics. Averroes is considered the father of secular thought in Western Europe and was influenced by Aristotelian Philosophy, and thus a major influence on the Roman Catholic theologian and saint, Thomas Aquinas.

Avicenna:
Lived c. 980 C.E. – 1037 C.E., was a Persian scholar and the greatest philosophy and physician of his time. His Arabic name was Ibn Sina.

Avicenna was a master in the fields of mathematics, physics, poetry, logic, and the sciences. Considered the father of modern medicine and clinical pharmacology, Avicenna was a pious Ismaili Shia Muslim.

Ayatollah Khomeini:
Lived 1902 C.E. – 1989 C.E., was an Iranian religious leader, politician, poet, and jurist. Khomeini was "a Marj'i al-Taqleed" or source of emulation. Known more for his political role, Khomeini is still loved by millions of Iranians. Imam Khomeini, as he is called in Iran, was vocally opposed to the "White Revolution" of the Shah of Iran in 1963, a decade after the CIA coup that removed the democratically elected president of Iran from office and reinstalled the Pehlavi dynasty to power. In 1964, Imam Khomeini denounced both the Shah and the United States because the Shah of Iran had granted diplomatic immunity to American military personnel in Iran. After the arrest of Khomeini, advisers to the Shah of Iran wanted to execute Ayatollah Khomeini, but the Shah refused, a decision which still grumbled about by former royalists now living abroad. Exiled for about a decade and a half from Iran, the Ayatollah Khomeini returned as a result of the popular and successful Islamic revolution that ousted the Shah of Iran. In the West, Ayatollah Khomeini is remembered for the crisis which came about when college students took hostage American Embassy workers because of CIA operation to overthrow the Islamic Government of Iran.

Buddha:
Died c. 400 B.C.E.?, usually refers to Siddhattha Gotama, who lived in the northern region of India, was the son of royalty, and founded the Buddhism. Most Buddhists consider Siddhattha to be the Supreme Buddha of Our Age. He is also referred to as Shakyamuni Buddha. It is said that Shakyamuni Buddha was born into a royal family and did not see suffering until after he married and fathered a son. When he first encountered suffering, the Buddha renounced the world and became an ascetic. Eventually, the Buddha attained enlightenment and began to preach the Four Noble Truths. The three main branches of Buddhism existing today are Theravada (The teachings of the Elders), Mahayana Buddhism (The Great Vehicle) which traditionally considered Theravada Buddhism as a lesser form of Buddhism (Hinayana Buddhism or The Lesser Vehicle), and Tibetan Buddhism, which is a more esoteric form of Mahayana Buddhism.

Charles Grandison Finney:
Lived 1792 C.E. – 1875 C.E., was an American Christian minister and revivalist during the Second Great Awakening, and is sometimes called "The Father of Modern Evangelism." Finney, who had studied and practiced Law,

introduced innovative practices in his Revival Meetings and was known for his extemporaneous preaching style. In the 1840s, Finney began teaching at Oberlin College in Ohio. Three of his well-known writings are: 1) Lectures on the Revival of Religion, 2) Systematic Theology, and his Memoirs. Although he came from a Calvinist background, Finney rejected the "Old Divinity" and stressed the Freedom of the Will, the Justice of God (theodicy) and rejected the Calvinist view of Original Sin and the Total Depravity of Man.

Charles Haddon Spurgeon:
Lived 1834 C.E. – 1892 C.E., was an English Baptist preacher, called both "The heir of the Puritans" and "The Prince of Preachers." Despite struggling with depression throughout his life, Spurgeon was known to preach as many as 10 sermons a week at different locations, and his sermons were translated into many different languages. Called to a pastorate at the age of 19, only 4 years after his conversion, Spurgeon preached at the New Park Street Chapel in Southwark, London, which was famous for its history of famous Particular/Calvinist Baptist pastors. Later, as his congregation grew, Spurgeon moved to the Metropolitan Tabernacle, which seated five thousand and could accommodate One thousand more with standing room. Spurgeon became involved in the "Downgrade" controversy after an article criticizing some Evangelical Baptist preachers for "down-grading" the Bible and the doctrine of Sola Scripture (The Bible Alone). Spurgeon's legacy lives on in the Reformed Baptist movement.

Fatima Al-Zahra:
Lived c. 605 or 615 C.E. – 632 C.E., was the daughter of Prophet Muhammad (PBUH) by his first wife Khadija Al-Kubra and is considered one of the best women by Muslims, and is considered one of the infallibles by most Shia Muslims. After the move to Medina, Fatima married the cousin of the Prophet, Ali Ibn Abu Talib, who was the 3rd Caliph and, for Shia Muslims, the first Imam. Fatima had three children with her husband Ali, including the 2nd Shia Imam Hassan Ibn Ali, the 3rd Imam Hussein Ibn Ali, and Zainab, all three of whom were martyred at the order of Caliphs. Fatima Al-Zahra died a short time after her Father, and Shias believed this happened while defending he husband Ali Ibn Talib from an attack by the future 2nd caliph Caliph Omar. Previous to this event, Fatima Al-Zahra requested from Caliph Abu Bakr her inheritance from her father, a piece of land called Fadak. However, Abu Bakr refused, citing a tradition alleged from The Prophet that children of prophets receive no inheritance… Shia sources state that Fatima never spoke to Abu Bakr again, but Sunni sources say she did. Shias also believe that no such tradition was ever uttered by the Prophet, so Abu Bakr was wrong to

deny Fatima's request. Fatima Al-Zahra was buried in Medina, though the actual site of her grave is unknown.

George Whitfield:

Lived 1714-1770, was an Anglican priest and revivalist speaker in the Calvinist/Reformed wing of the early Methodist movement during the First Great Awakening… Whitfield's Calvinist theology was at odds with that of his friend, John Wesley, the founder of the Methodist movement. Whitfield preached successfully in England and the United States of America.

Geza Vermes Living:

Born 1924 C.E., is a Jewish Hungarian scholar, well-known writer on Jewish and Christian subjects, an Aramaic scholar, and one of the original Dead Sea Scrolls researchers. Geza Vermes is considered the greatest Jesus scholar in modern times in some quarters. He converted to Christianity and became a Roman Catholic priest, but reverted to Judaism in 1957, moved to England, joined the faculty at Oxford, and eventually became the first Oxford's Jewish Studies professor, a post he held until his retirement in 1991.

Hugo Grotius:

Lived 1583 C.E. – 1685 C.E., was a Dutch jurist and one of the architects of international law, which he based on natural law. He was, among other things, a philosopher, theologian, and disciple of Dutch theologian Jacob Arminius. When the followers of Arminius staged the Remonstrance against the Calvinist, Grotius was imprisoned, but escaped to Paris and is considered a hero today in the Netherlands because of this escape. A writer of important books on Law and Theology, Grotius was read and admired by such figures as the Swedish King Gustavus Adolphus.

Hussein:

Imam Hussein Lived 626 C.E. – 680 C.E., was the 2nd son of Imam Ali Ibn Abu Talib by Fatima Al-Zahra, and thus the grandson of the Prophet Muhammad and 3rd Imam of Shia Muslims. Imam Hussein and all male members of his family except one were martyred by the army of Yazid Ibn Muhawiya Ibn Abu Sufyan at the Battle of Karbala on the 10th of Muharram, 61 Hijr/680 C.E. This was because Yazid would not allow Imam Hussein and his family to go into exiles, but demanded an oath of fealty or death. The only male to survive the battle of Karbala was the son of Imam Hussein, the 4th Imam Al-Sajjad.

Hyam Maccoby:

Lived 1924 C.E. – 2004 C.E., was a British Jewish Scholar noted for his theories about the historical Jesus and the motives of the Apostle Paul.

Maccoby wrote extensively on Anti-Semitism in the history of Christianity, as well as the history of the Jewish Religion and Talmudic studies.

Idries Shah:
Lived 1923 or 24 C.E. – 1996 C.E., was an Afghan-Irish writer and teacher of Sufism. Born in India and a descendant of a family of Afghan nobles, Shah grew up in England. He presented Sufism as a universal vehicle of wisdom that pre-dated Islam which adapted itself to the current circumstances of time, place and culture. Shah published translations of stories and sayings, and wrote books on psychology from the perspective of Sufism.

Jacob Arminius:
Lived 1560 C.E. to 1609 C.E., was a Dutch Theologian who respected the Theology of John Calvin but disagreed on the issues of Irresistible Grace, Unconditional Election and Perseverance of the Saints. His students in Holland held the Remonstrance which led the Calvinists to define the Canons of Dordt, from which the 5 Points of Calvinism are culled. John Wesley held to the theology of Arminius.

James Robson:
A western Scholar of Islam who published a compilation of the traditions of Jesus Christ (PBUH) from Sunni and Sufi sources.

John Calvin:
Lived 1509 C.E. – 1564 C.E, and along with Martin Luther, one of the most important theologians of the Protestant Reformation. Calvin fled France and was invited to Geneva, Switzerland by William Farel to help reform the Church in that city. Calvin's most famous publication was his Institutes of the Christian Religion, which saw four editions before reaching it final form. The Reformed Theology of the Puritans comes from Calvinism.

John Cassian:
Lived 360 C.E. – 435 C.E., was a monk, mystic, and theologian and was canonized a Catholic Saint. Cassian entered the Augustinian – Pelagius debate and reached his own conclusions on the effect of sin on man, and his views were accepted by the Eastern Church. Cassian is known as one of the Scythian Monks and one of the Desert Fathers. His writings influenced Saint Benedict the monk and his "Rule" for monks.

John Wesley:
Lived 1703 C.E. – 1791 C.E. was an Anglican Priest, founding member of the Methodist Movement in the Anglican Church, and ordained the first bishop of the Methodist Church after not finding a Bishop willing to ordain priests

from Candidates in the Methodist Movement. Wesley, along with his brother Charles, and George Whitfield, was part of the Holy Club while attending Oxford College. Wesley followed the lead of George Whitfield and held open-air meetings of an evangelical nature that were highly successful. Wesley and his Methodist movement also took on social justice issues of his time. Wesley, holding to Arminian theology, was at odds with George Whitfield's Calvinist views. Though they could not work together, they respected each other as Christians.

Jonathan Edwards:
Lived 1702 C.E. – 1758 C.E., was an early American Congregationalist preacher and Calvinist theologian. Edwards was also a missionary to Native Americans. He is known for his sermon, later titled "Sinner's in the Hands of an Angry God," which stressed the just wrath of God against sin and also demonstrated the Providence of God in Salvation. Odd behaviors on the part of the audience caused controversy for Edwards over the "bodily effects of the Holy Spirit" during his preaching. Edwards was one of the greatest preachers of the First Great Awakening, writing many sermons, as well as Essays and books. Edwards is considered by many to be the greatest Theologian America has ever produced.

Marcion:
Lived c.85 C.E. – 160 C.E., was an Early Church leader and theologian who was excommunicated by the early church at Rome as a heretic. Marcion's movement would rival that of the proto-Orthodox church for the next few centuries. Marcion taught that there were two Gods, one (Yahweh) evil toward man because of sin. The Heavenly Father, however, showed his compassion by sending Jesus Christ to save mankind, and Paul as his chief Apostle. The New Testament canon used by Marcion included an edited version of the Gospel of Luke called The Gospel of Marcion, and Ten Epistles by Paul.

Martin Luther:
Lived 1483 C.E. – 1546 C.E., in Germany, was an Augustinian Monk, theologian, professor, priest, and reformer in the Roman Catholic Church who became the Father of the Protestant Reformation. Luther came to believe that salvation was by the grace of God alone, a free gift, and that sinners were justified by faith alone by faith in Jesus Christ alone as Redeemer from the bondage and guilt of sin. As a monk, Luther was obsessed with the problem of forgiveness of sin and went to confession often as a result, devoting himself to fasting, prayer. His superior ordered that Luther become an academic, and as a result Luther was ordained a priest and later was awarded Doctor of

Theology degree from the University of Wittenberg and joined the faculty of the University in the position of Doctor of Bible, where Luther remained for the rest of his teaching career. Luther became concerned with the selling of indulgences, especially as they were advertized by Johann Tetzel, a Dominican priest. As a result, he nailed the 95 Theses on the door of the church in Wittenberg, a common practice of the time, to discuss what Luther saw as abuses in the sale of indulgences. However, the 95 Theses, which were written in Latin, were translated into German and published as a tract. Luther eventually came to believe that the Roman Catholic Church was in need of a major reformation, and so when threatened with excommunication, he broke with the Church. More writings were published by Luther and in 1520, Luther was finally excommunicated. Luther himself considered his book The Bondage of the Will, and his Catechism to be his greatest writings. Other writings of note are the Smalcald Articles, three works from 1520 entitled: To the Christian Nobility of the German Nation, On the Babylonian Captivity of the Church, and On the Freedom of a Christian. Luther also is known for his German Translation of the Bible and his commentaries on the Pauline epistles of Romans and Galatians. Luther also reformed the liturgical use in Germany.

Montanus:
An early 2nd Century C.E. Christian leader considered a heretic by proto-Orthodox Christians. The sect led by Montanus flourished in Asia Minor in Phrygia. In isolated locations, Montanism existed into the 8th Century C.E. Montanus believed he was the promised Comforter spoken of in John's Gospel, chapter 14 through 16. As a result, he believed the doctrines he taught fulfilled and superseded the teachings of the Apostles. Montanus encouraged ecstatic utterances and prophesying, and those who rejected the teachings of Montanus were considered to have sinned in such a way as to never be able to be saved. Montanus taught that any Christian who fell from grace could not be redeemed, and thus anyone who divorced and remarried was lost forever. Montanus also predicted that Jesus Christ would return to the village of Pepuza to set up the New Jerusalem, but Monatus died and the prediction did not come to pass. After the death of Montanus, the sect regrouped and de-emphasized the prophetical aspects of the movement, which some modern Christians believe are present in the modern Charismatic and Pentecostal Movements.

Muhammad:
Prophet Muhammad (PBUH) Lived c. 570 C.E. – 632 C.E., is the founder of the religion of Islam and considered by Muslims to be a Prophet and Messenger

of God. The Seal of all Prophets and Messengers. A descendant of Christians and other Monotheists and living in Mecca in Arabia, Muhammad married Khadijah at about age 25 and began his mission at age 40. Muhammad preached the Oneness and Unity of God and Submission to and Peace with God. In the first few years, Muhammad preached only to close family, and then to close friends, and finally to the city of Mecca, where the Arabs came every year to worship their idols in the Kaaba, the House of God which Prophet Abraham built for Prophet Ishmael and his descendants after Ishmael was separated from the camp of Abraham and Sarah. Muhammad invited the Meccans to remove the idols and worship God alone. Muhmmad's message also appealed to the poor of Mecca who were victims of the tribal system of the Arabian dark ages. The merchants of Mecca came to persecute Muhammad and his followers, so he sent some Muslims to live in Ethiopia where they were accepted by the Negus, the King of Ethiopia. Eventually, Muhammad's message was received by some of the citizens of the City of Yathraib, which was eventually renamed the City of the Prophet, or just the City (Medina) for short. Many Muslims moved to Medina. Finally, there was an attempt to assassinate the Prophet by representatives of various tribes (as the Prophet's protector, his uncle Talib, had passed away). The Prophet left Mecca for Medina while his would-be assassins came to his bed, only to find his cousin and future son-in-law Ali Ibn Abu Talib in the bed. Once in Medina, the first Islamic State was established. The Constitution of Medina declared that the three Jewish tribes be treated as brothers. The merchants of Mecca responded by seizing the property of the Muslims and persecuting those Muslims who stayed alive. The Meccans first attacked the Muslims at the Battle of Badr, which was won by the Muslims and allowed Muhammad to make treaties with certain Bedouin tribes. At the battle of Uhud, victory was snatched from the Muslims because of a lack of discipline by archers, most of whom left their station to take war booty. Hamzah the uncle of the Prophet was killed at Uhud. In the battle of the Trench, Mecca laid siege to Medina, where a defensive trench was built by the suggestion of the Persian Muslim Salman Al-Farsi. Treachery by one of the Jewish tribes almost brought defeat to the Muslims. Finally, sometime after this battle, Muhammad led the Muslims to the pilgrimage to Mecca. Because the Muslims were unarmed and on Pilgrimage, the Meccan leaders could not attack them without losing their reputation as guardians of the Kaaba. Eventually, an agreement was reached between Muhammad and the Meccans that allowed the Muslims to return the next year for the Pilgrimage, though the Muslims could not attend that year. This treaty allowed the Muslims to spread their religion throughout the Arabian Penninsula and enter into treaties. After two years, agents of the Meccans broke the treaty. This allowed the Muslims to march on Mecca.

Abu Sufyan, a leader of the Merchants in Mecca, went out to meet the approaching Muslim army and declare the Muslim statement of belief. When the Muslims reached Mecca, it was announced that non-Muslims should stay inside their homes. The Kaaba was cleansed by the removal of the idols. Eventually, the Muslims won the war against what was left of the coalition who had sided with the Meccans. At the event of Al-Qadeer, Muhammad preached his final sermon where he declared his mission had been completed. According to traditions considered authentic by Sunni Scholars, Muhammad left "two weighty things" to the Muslims to guide them after his passing from the scene: the Quran (the book of Revelations given by the Prophet from God during his mission) and his family. Other Sunni traditions not considered authentic by Sunni scholars state that the Prophet said he left "The Quran and Sunnah" and "The Quran alone." Shia Muslims believe that the tradition considered authentic by Sunni scholars is the true account of the event. Muhammad in his time was a statesman, merchant, orator, legislator, social reformer, philosopher, and military general, and according to Muslims, the Prophet and Messenger of God.

Muhammad bin Abdul Wahab Al-Najdi:
Lived 1703 C.E. – 1792 C.E., was an Arab Scholar born in Najd, from whom comes the Western name of the movement he founded, the Wahhabi Movement. Those who follow the teachings of Bin Abdul Wahab do not call themselves by this name. Accounts of his life state that he studied with his father, and then with scholars in Basra, and later allied himself to the House of Saud. Ibn Abdul Wahab, like most scholars from Najd, followed the Hanbali School of Jurisprudence. Ibn Abdul Wahab's strict version of Hanbali Jurisprudence believed in purified Islam from Shirk and Innovation. He first implemented his teachings by having the grave of a companion of the Prophet leveled because visits made to the grave by locals were considered by him to be "grave worship." Second, he wanted to have an adulteress stoned despite the Quranic penalty of 40 lashings. His pact with the House of Saud led to missionary activity for the Salafi Movement and as the Saudis conquered the Arabian Penninsula, they brought the teachings of Ibn Abdul Wahab to the conquered areas. Modern Salafi and Wahhabi movements are direct descendants of his movement.

Paul of Tarsus, the Apostle:
Lived c.64-65? C.E., is considered by Protestant Christians to be the foremost Apostle of Christ despite not being one of the original 12 Apostles nor being chosen as a replacement by the Apostles after the betrayal by Judas Iscariot. Paul considered himself a Jew of the sect of the Pharisees who was given power

by the Sadducee High Priest to persecute and arrest Christians. The New Testament book of Acts of the Apostles states that Paul, then named Saul, watched and agreed with the stoning of the deacon Stephen. Later, while on the way to Damascus, Paul said he saw a bright light and was knocked off his horse and heard the voice of Jesus Christ. Paul was blinded but eventually was healed by a Christian named Cornelius and became a devout Christian. After some years, Paul became a missionary to the Gentiles. The New Testament described 4 missionary journeys on which Paul spread the Gospel of "Christ Crucified" and planted epistles. Thirteen letters to these churches are included, plus the letter to the Hebrews which was included on Paul's authority, although it was probably not written by him. It is said that Paul was martyred by the Roman Emperor Nero. Paul, along with Simon Peter, are considered the Holy Apostles who founded the Church of Rome by the Roman Catholic Church. Most Protestants would say Paul was the greatest of the Apostles. Gnostic Christians in the early Church also afforded Paul a high place. According to early Christian writings, the Ebionite Christians, declared Judaizers and a heretical sect by the Gentile Church, believed Paul became a Sadducee due to his desire to marry the daughter of the High Priest of the Temple of Jerusalem, but when Paul was rejected by the daughter of the High Priest, Paul left Judaism to become a Christian. The New Testament describes controversy between Paul and Judaizing Christians that even caused a controversy between Paul and the Apostle Peter. However, the Second Epistle attributed to Peter describes Paul's writings as scripture, which some twist to their destruction.

Peter The Apostle:
Lived c.1 C.E. – 64 C.E., was the leader of the 12 Apostles chosen by Jesus Christ and an early Church leader. According to Catholic tradition, Peter was the first Bishop of Rome and is a canonized saint. The Gospels describe Peter as a fisherman from Galilee. Jesus Christ tells Peter in the Gospels that Peter and his companions would become "fishers of men." Peter is said to be the spokesman of the Apostles, sometimes beginning in boldness but losing his composure afterward, as when Peter walked on water toward Jesus Christ, but then looked away and went down into the water, only to be saved by the hand Jesus Christ. It is written that Peter claimed he would never deny Jesus Christ at the Last Supper, but after the arrest of Jesus Christ, Peter denied him three times. After the Ascension of Jesus Christ, on the Day of Pentecost, tongues of fire appeared on the heads of the Apostles. They began speaking and Jews from other lands could understand the words in their mother languages. After this event, Peter becomes a bold and valiant worker for Gospel, except for the controversy over the Gentiles with Paul. Christian tradition states

that when Peter was to be executed by the Romans, he didn't believe he was worthy of the same method of execution as his Savior, and so this tradition claims Peter was crucified upside-down.

Puritans:
Protestants from England who sought to purify the Anglican Church in its worship and doctrine. It was a pejorative term given these Reformers by their critics. The Puritans wanted the English Church to be more in line with the Reformed Churches on the Continent. The Puritan movement can be traced back to the reign of King Edward VI but the term was not coined until after 1560 to describe those who wanted the state church to go farther in its reforms than was allowed by the Elizabethan Religious settlement of 1559. Puritans were Calvinist in doctrine. The divines who worked on the Westminster Standards (Reformed Catechisms, The Confession of Faith, and other documents) were Puritans. Puritans came to the American colonies and heavily influenced the religious environment of the Colonial America and the Early United States. The American Theologian and Evangelist Jonathan Edwards was considered a beneficiary of Puritan thought. In England, the Baptist Minister Charles Haddon Spurgeon, considered the Prince of Preacher, was considered an heir of the Puritans.

R. A. Torrey:
Lived 1856 C.E. – 1928 C.E., full name Reuben Archer Torrey, was an American Pastor, Evangelist, and author of over 40 books, including What The Bible Teachers, How To Pray, and Torrey's Topical Textbook. A graduate of Yale Divinity School, who also studied in Europe at the Universities of Leipzig and Erlangen, Torrey became a co-worker with the famous American Evangelist Dwight L. Moody.

Rashad Khalifa:
Lived 1935-1990, was an Egyptian-American biochemist who founded United Submitters International, and was assassinated while in his office in the Submitters Mosque in Tucson Arizona. Khalifa believed that although he was not the last Prophet, he was the last Messenger. He used English terms instead of Arabic terms, thus his Religion was Submission, not Islam, and thus he was a Submitter, not a Muslim. Khalifa discovered for himself, using a computer, that the word God appears in the Quran a multiple of 19 times, and that the Bismillah (stated before all Surahs of the Quran except Surah 9) had 19 letters. Another Surah has a second Bismillah, so the number of Bismillahs in the Quran is a multiple of 19. This much had been taught by some Muslims in past centuries. With the use of a computer, Khalifa was able to find more

words that occurred in the Quran in multiples of the number 19. This led him to declare the Miracle 19 Code of the Quran. Eventually, Khalifa came to doubt that the last two verses of Surah 9 were authentic. He removed those verses and used another variant word to keep the count of occurrences of the word God as a multiple of the number 19. At this point, Khalifa declared that traditions were fabrications and that only the Quran alone should be used by Submitters. Khalifa declared himself a Messenger, and taught that one had to believe this to be saved. Khalifa believed his mission was to restore the used of the purified Quran alone. After his death, his movement split into other sects and groups, many of which no longer taught that Khalifa was the last messenger and also restored the final two verses to Surah 9, but still wish to use the Quran alone.

Shah of Iran:
The title given to the King of Iran in the Farsi language. The final Shah of Iran, Muhammad Reza Shah Pahlavi, was exiled from Iran by the popular Islamic Revolution, at which time Iran became an Islamic Republic in 1979 C.E.

Tarif Khalidi:
Professor at the American University of Beirut. Khalidi published an excellent compilation of about 300 Muslim traditions of the sayings of Jesus Christ from Muslim sources. His book is titled "The Muslim Jesus."

Tertullian:
Lived c.120 C.E. – c. 220 C.E., full Latin name Quintus Septimius Florens Tertullianus, was a controversial early Christian writer, and the first "Latin" Church father. Tertullian is most famous for coining the term Trinity (Latin: Trinitas) and giving the first theological exposition of the Trinitarian formula. In later life, Tertullian became a Montanist and eventually left the sect to form his group. Tertullian also wrote writings on moral subjects and against heresies.

Thomas Jefferson:
Lived 1743 C.E. – 1826 C.E., was the Third American President. Theologically, Jefferson was a Deist and a Unitarian who did not believe in the Deity of Jesus Christ, the Virgin Birth, nor the miracles attributed to Jesus Christ in the Bible, and did not believe Jesus rose from the dead. However, Thomas Jefferson admired the moral teachings of Jesus. The Jefferson Bible is compilation of the moral teachings of Jesus Christ which Jefferson read devotionally. In a letter from 1825, Jefferson wrote: "I am anxious to see the doctrine of one

god commenced in our state. But the population of my neighborhood is too slender, and is too much divided into other sects to maintain any one preacher well. I must therefore be contented to be a Unitarian by myself, although I know there are many around me who would become so, if once they could hear the questions fairly stated..."

LaVergne, TN USA
15 September 2009
157866LV00002BB/2/P